THE GREAT MOLASSES FLOOD, 1919

PHOTOS ©: 150: AUTHOR PHOTO; 151 TOP: STEPHEN BARNES/GETTY IMAGES; 151 CENTER LEFT: KIRN VINTAGE STOCK/CORBIS/GETTY IMAGES; 151 CENTER RIGHT: COPYRIGHT SOUTHERN CALIFORNIA EDISON 2024. USED WITH PERMISSION OF SOUTHERN CALIFORNIA EDISON; 151 BOTTOM: THE PROTECTED ART ARCHIVE/ALAMY STOCK PHOTO; 152 TOP LEFT: CHRONICLE/ALAMY STOCK PHOTO; 152 TOP RIGHT: GL ARCHIVE/ALAMY STOCK PHOTO; 152 BOTTOM: VINTAGE_SPACE/ALAMY STOCK PHOTO; 153 TOP: APIC/GETTY IMAGES; 153 CENTER, 153 BOTTOM: COURTESY OF THE BOSTON PUBLIC LIBRARY, LESLIE JONES COLLECTION; 154 TOP: LIBRARY OF CONGRESS; 154 BOTTOM LEFT, 154 BOTTOM RIGHT: COURTESY OF THE BOSTON PUBLIC LIBRARY, LESLIE JONES COLLECTION; 155 TOP: THE BOSTONIAN SOCIETY/WIKIMEDIA; 155 CENTER LEFT: COURTESY OF THE BOSTON PUBLIC LIBRARY, BOSTON PICTORIAL ARCHIVE; 155 CENTER RIGHT: FINE ART IMAGES/BRIDGEMAN IMAGES; 155 BOTTOM LEFT: THE BOSTON GLOBE; 155 BOTTOM RIGHT: AMPHOTORA/GETTY IMAGES; 156 TOP: CAIA IMAGE/SCIENCE SOURCE; 156 CENTER: SHUTTERSTOCK.COM; 156 BOTTOM: PGIAM/GETTY IMAGES.

SPECIAL THANKS TO STEPHEN PULEO

LIBRARY OF CONGRESS CONTROL NUMBER AVAILABLE
ISBN 978-93-5954-318-5

PRINTED IN INDIA AT: VK GLOBAL DIGITAL PRIVATE LIMITED
THIS REPRINT EDITION, JULY 2025
EDITED BY KATIE WOEHR
LETTERING BY JANICE CHIANG
INKS BY KAREN DE LA VEGA
COLOR BY NEDA KAZEMIFAR
BOOK DESIGN BY KATIE FITCH AND BECKY JAMES
CREATIVE DIRECTOR: YAFFA JASKOLL

WEDNESDAY, JANUARY 15, 1919
12:30 p.m.
The North End, Boston
RUMBLE
RUMBLE
SPLOOOSH
RUMBLE RUMBLE RUMBLE RUMBLE RUMBLE

RUMBLE
RUMBLE
RUMBLE
RUMBLE
RUMBLE
RUMBLE

UNNH

WHAT DO WE DO?

TONY! GRAB THAT!

WATCH OUT!
CRRRRRRRRRRACK
CARMEN!
TONY'S VOICE IS THE LAST SOUND I HEAR—
—BEFORE THE MOLASSES SWALLOWS ME WHOLE.

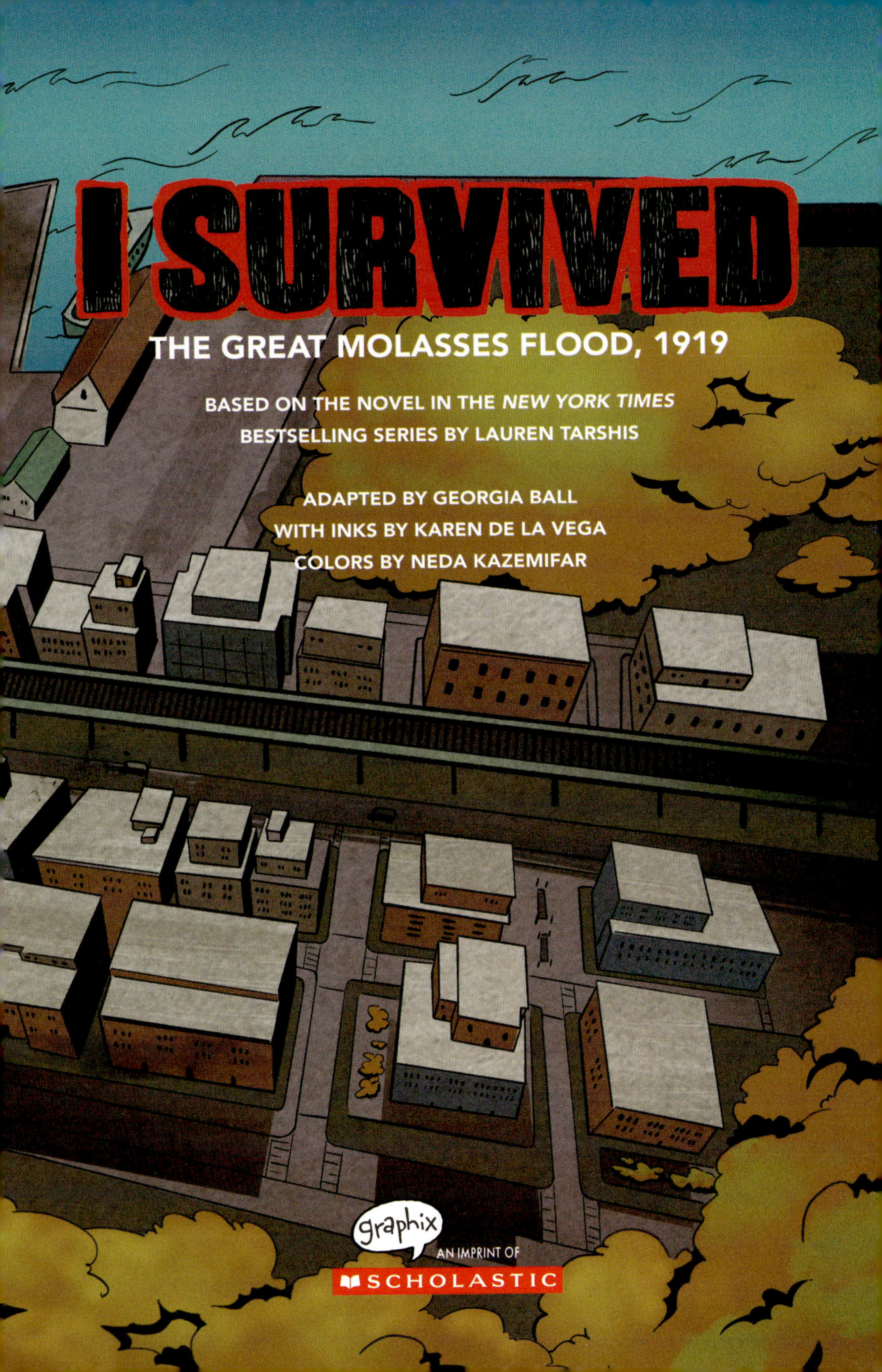
I SURVIVED
THE GREAT MOLASSES FLOOD, 1919
BASED ON THE NOVEL IN THE *NEW YORK TIMES*
BESTSELLING SERIES BY LAUREN TARSHIS
ADAPTED BY GEORGIA BALL
WITH INKS BY KAREN DE LA VEGA
COLORS BY NEDA KAZEMIFAR
graphix
AN IMPRINT OF
SCHOLASTIC

Three and a half months earlier
FRIDAY, SEPTEMBER 27, 1918
The North End, Boston

ARE YOU SURE YOU DON'T WANT TO STOP AT THE BAKERY?
MR. ORTELLI MIGHT GIVE US A FREE CANNOLI TO SHARE... 
GET YOUR PAPER! DEADLY FLU KILLS HUNDREDS!

I KNOW IT'S NEVER WORKED BEFORE, BUT WE CAN ALWAYS TRY . . .
NOT TODAY, CARMEN.

ALL RIGHT, WHAT'S WRONG?
MR. LAWRENCE ***HATES*** ME!

HE DOESN'T ***HATE*** YOU, TONY.
YES, HE DOES!

HE THINKS I'M STUPID.
I AM STUPID.
NO, YOU'RE NOT.
ALL HE HAS TO DO IS STUDY HARDER . . .
OR OPEN A BOOK, FOR ONCE!

IF THIS IS ABOUT THAT F ON YOUR MATH TEST—
OH, I'VE HAD PLENTY OF THOSE.

BUT HE KEPT ME IN AT RECESS TO PLAY BORING MATH GAMES!

OUR TEACHER IS TRYING TO *TORTURE* ME!
MR. LAWRENCE IS ONLY TRYING TO HELP.

HE COULD HELP BY GIVING US AN EASIER TEST.
THAT TEST WAS IMPOSSIBLE!
HMMM . . . I GOT A PERFECT SCORE.

A
I'M HIDING MY TEST FROM TONY.

WE LEFT OUR LITTLE VILLAGE IN ITALY FOUR YEARS AGO.

OUR ANCESTORS HAD LIVED THERE FOR HUNDREDS OF YEARS.

BUT WHEN I WAS TWO, IN 1908, A POWERFUL EARTHQUAKE STRUCK SOUTHERN ITALY.
ENTIRE CITIES TURNED TO DUST.

A GIANT TIDAL WAVE SWEPT ACROSS THE LAND.
MORE THAN 100,000 PEOPLE DIED...

INCLUDING MAMA.

I HAVE ONLY A FLASH OF MEMORY FROM THAT TERRIBLE DAY.

IT'S DIM AND HAZY—LIKE A DREAM.
THE SOUND OF PAPA'S VOICE . . .
HOLD ON!
THE ROARING WAVES . . .

THE SCREAMS OF THE PEOPLE AROUND US . . .
WHAP

PAPA NEVER TALKS ABOUT THE EARTHQUAKE.

IN ITALY, REMINDERS WERE EVERYWHERE.

I WANT TO STAY, BUT THERE'S NO FUTURE FOR CARMEN HERE.
THE SCHOOL STILL HASN'T OPENED. IT'S GETTING HARDER TO EARN MONEY AND BUY FOOD . . .
THEN YOU KNOW WHAT YOU MUST DO.

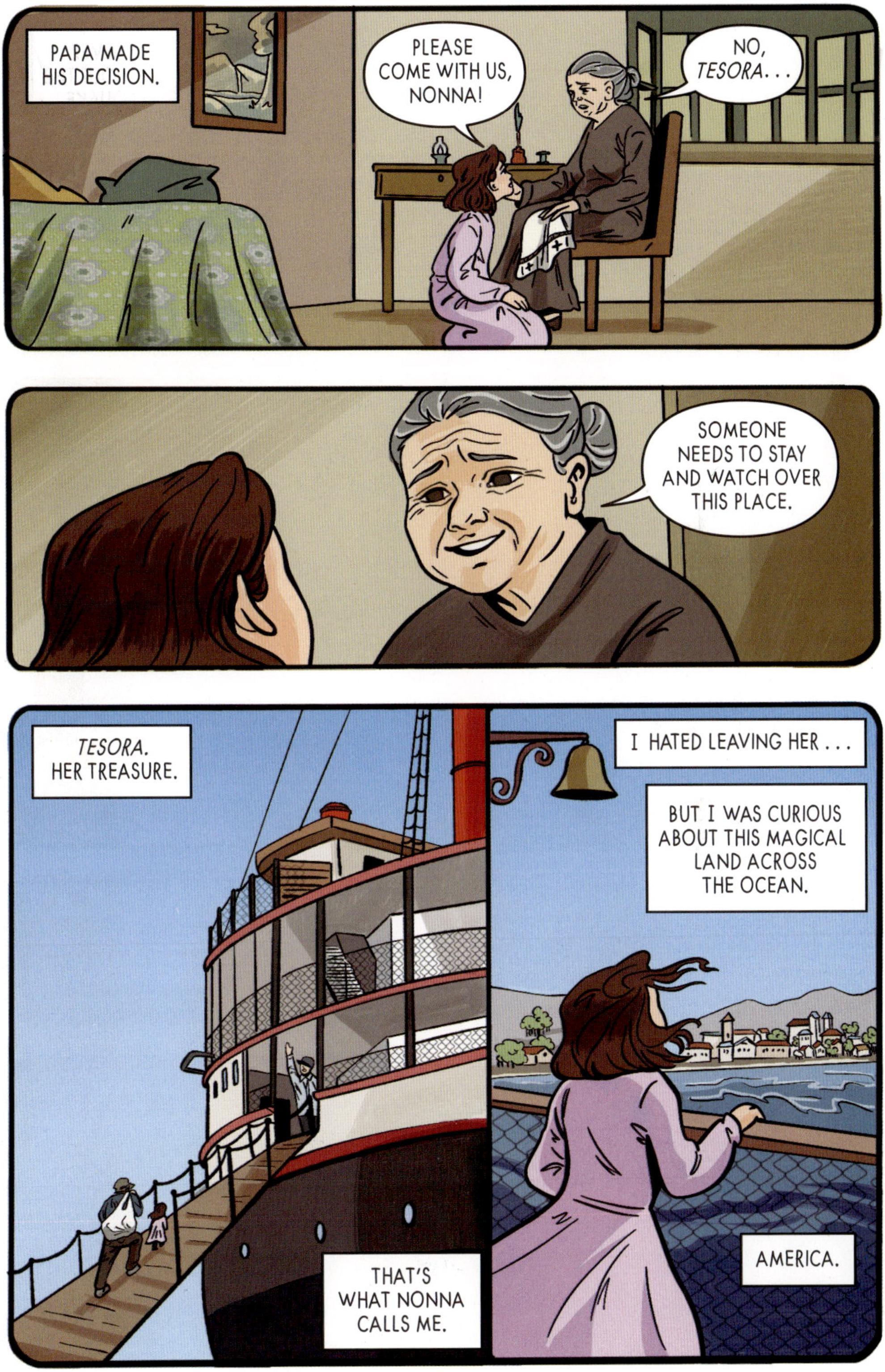

TESORA. HER TREASURE.

THAT'S WHAT NONNA CALLS ME.

I HATED LEAVING HER . . .

BUT I WAS CURIOUS ABOUT THIS MAGICAL LAND ACROSS THE OCEAN.

AMERICA.

LIFE WOULD BE EASIER IN *L'AMERICA*. . .

IMAGINE MY SHOCK WHEN WE ARRIVED IN THE NORTH END.

THERE'S BARELY ENOUGH ROOM IN OUR APARTMENT FOR ME, PAPA—
—AND THE FAMILY OF RATS THAT REFUSES TO LEAVE.

"WHAT WAS PAPA THINKING, NONNA?
"WHY WOULD ANYONE WANT TO LIVE IN AMERICA?

"WE MADE A MISTAKE!"
"BE PATIENT, *TESORA* . . .

"TREES DON'T GROW OVERNIGHT."
WHY IS NONNA WRITING ABOUT TREES?

THERE ARE HARDLY ANY TREES IN THE NORTH END, BUT LIKE TREES . . .
PAPA AND I SLOWLY GREW INTO OUR LIVES IN BOSTON.

SOMETIMES I PRETEND I'M BACK IN MY OLD VILLAGE...
SMELLING LEMONS, FLOWERS, AND SEA SALT IN THE BREEZE.

BUT THE NORTH END IS MY HOME NOW.

OUR NEIGHBORS ARE LIKE FAMILY.
MOST NIGHTS WE JOIN THE GRASSOS UPSTAIRS FOR HOMEMADE PASTA OR SOUP.

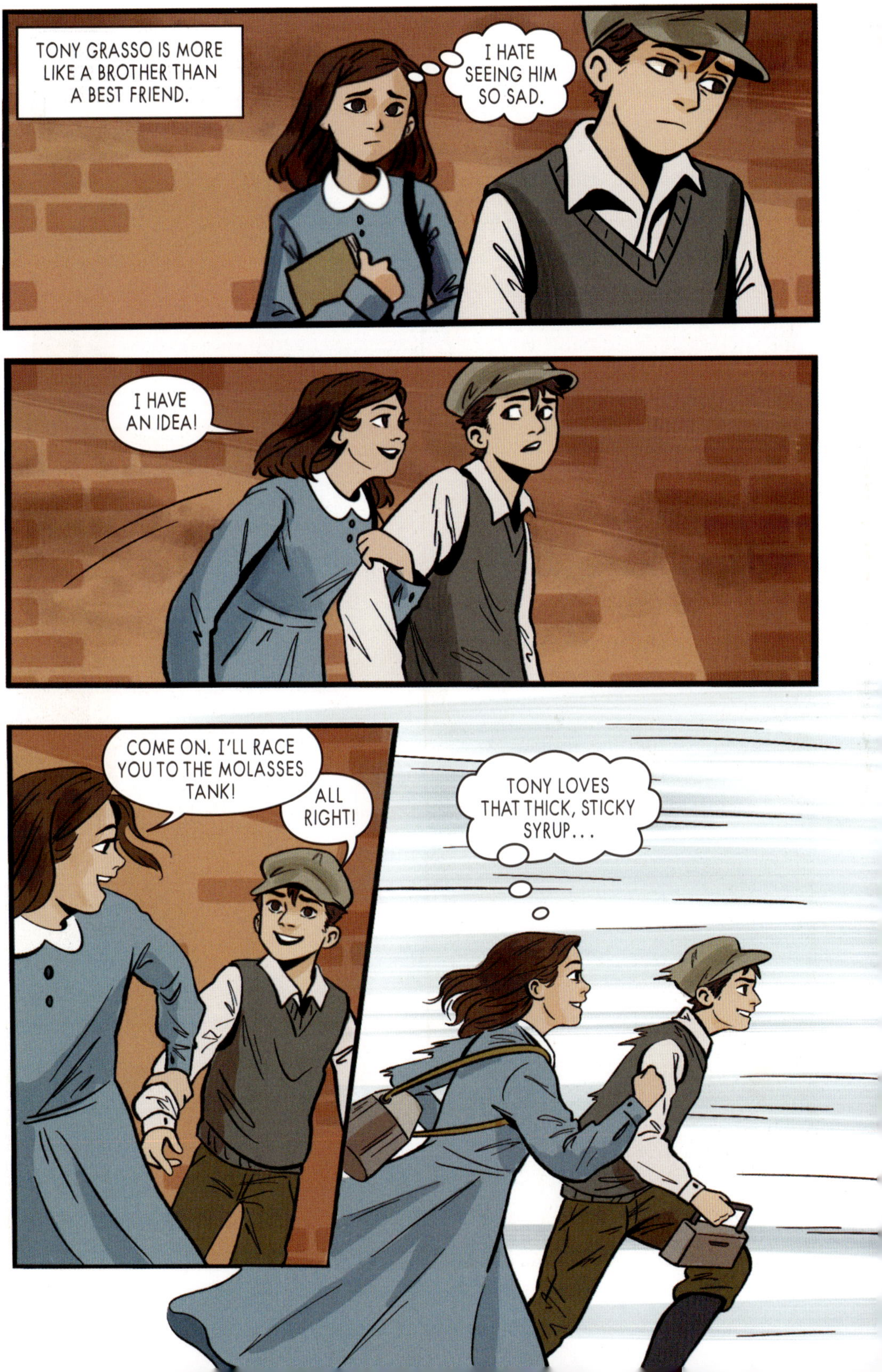

COME ON. I'LL RACE YOU TO THE MOLASSES TANK!

ALL RIGHT!

TONY LOVES THAT THICK, STICKY SYRUP...

I THOUGHT YOU HATED MOLASSES!
IT'S NOT MY FAVORITE...
MAYBE I'LL TAKE SOME TO ROSIE.

ROSIE IS THE OLD MARE WHO LIVES AT THE STABLE WHERE PAPA WORKS.

I RIDE HER TO THE PARK AND WRITE LETTERS TO NONNA.
NONNA LOVES HEARING ABOUT TONY.
SHE CALLS HIM *TROTTOLINO*—WILD BOY.

I CAN SEE THE MOLASSES LEAKING OUT OF THE TANK FROM HERE.
WHY WASTE A PENNY AT THE CANDY STORE WHEN YOU CAN GET A TASTE OF MOLASSES FOR FREE?

SLAP
SLAP

I WIN!
I KNEW THE TANK WOULD CHEER HIM UP!

IT'S LEAKING MORE THAN EVER TODAY.
SURE IS!

MMM, TASTES LIKE CRACKER JACK.

BLECH IT ALWAYS REMINDS ME OF BLACK LICORICE.

HELLO, I'M MR. LAWRENCE.
RECESS IS NOW AGAINST THE LAW.
HEE-HEE

LET'S FIND SOME STICKS TO PUT IT ON.
THAT'S ENOUGH FOR ME, THANKS.

BEING THIS CLOSE TO THE TANK ALWAYS MAKES ME QUEASY.

WHY DO YOU THINK THE TANK LEAKS SO MUCH?
WHOEVER BUILT IT DID A BAD JOB, I GUESS.

IT BLOCKS OUT THE SUN AND RUINS THE VIEW. WHY DO THEY NEED SO MUCH MOLASSES ANYWAY?
OH, RIGHT. I TRY SO HARD NOT TO THINK ABOUT IT, I ALWAYS FORGET...

I HEARD PAPA'S BOSS, MR. VITA, TALKING ABOUT IT . . .
THEY SAY THE TANK CAN HOLD MORE THAN TWO MILLION GALLONS.

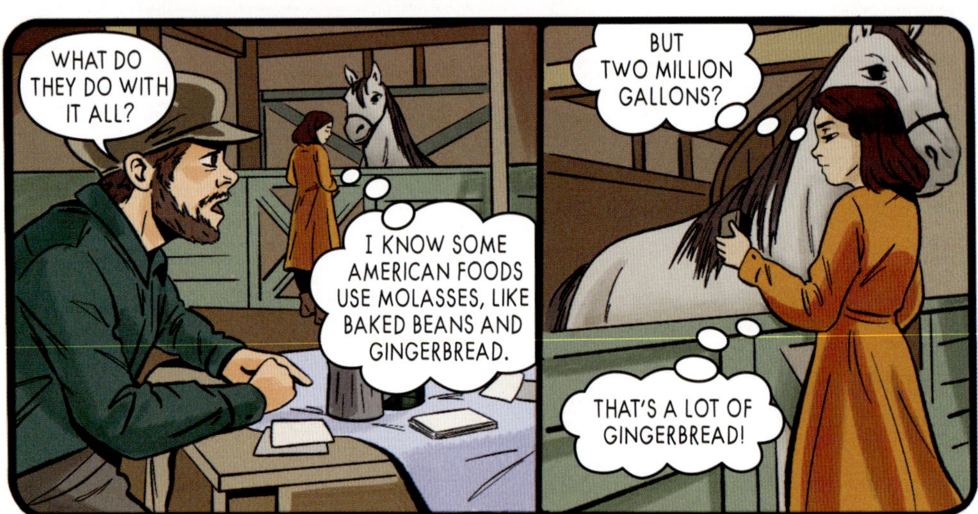
WHAT DO THEY DO WITH IT ALL?
I KNOW SOME AMERICAN FOODS USE MOLASSES, LIKE BAKED BEANS AND GINGERBREAD.
BUT TWO MILLION GALLONS?
THAT'S A LOT OF GINGERBREAD!

IT'S USED FOR BOMBS.
BOMBS?!
THEY SEND IT TO A FACTORY, BOIL IT DOWN—
—AND TURN IT INTO INDUSTRIAL ALCOHOL FOR BOMBS AND DYNAMITE.

JUST ONE OF THE MANY STRANGE THINGS ABOUT AMERICA THAT I CAN'T FIGURE OUT— OR COULDN'T, ONCE UPON A TIME.

THERE WAS EVEN A TIME WHEN I THOUGHT THE BOSTON RED SOX WERE SOCKS YOU WORE ON YOUR FEET!

THAT WAS A WHILE AGO, BEFORE AMERICA JOINED THE GREAT WAR.

THIS WAR HAS BEEN GOING ON FOR FOUR YEARS. AMERICA JOINED A YEAR AND A HALF AGO.
THERE ARE NEW WEAPONS IN THIS WAR.
MACHINE GUNS AND POISON GAS.

THOUSANDS OF AMERICAN SOLDIERS ARE DEAD.
MR. LAWRENCE CAME BACK FROM EUROPE WITH A LIMP.

HOW MANY PEOPLE GOT HURT—OR DIED—FROM BOMBS MADE WITH MOLASSES FROM THIS TANK?
SUDDENLY THIS TANK DOESN'T SEEM LIKE FUN ANYMORE.

HEY, YOU DONE YET?
JUST ONE MORE LICK AND—

GURRRR-GUH-GURRRRRR

IS IT DOGS?
GURRRR-GUH-GURRRRRRR

THE NORTH END IS INFESTED WITH VICIOUS STRAYS.

IF YOU GET BIT BY A DOG WITH RABIES, YOU'LL DIE IF YOU DON'T GET SHOTS IN YOUR STOMACH.

IT'S GETTING LOUDER . . .
THE GROUND IS SHAKING!
GUR
UG-GLUG-
RRRRRR
RUMBLE RUMBLE RUMBLE

IS IT AN EARTHQUAKE?
BUT I DIDN'T THINK WE HAD THOSE IN BOSTON . . .
RUMBLE RUMBLE RUMBLE RUMBLE

LOOK!
RUMBLE
RUMBLE
RUMBLE
RUMBLE

GURRRRR-GLUG-GLUG-GLUG-GUH-GURRRRRRR
RUMBLE
RUMBLE
RUMBLE
RUMBLE
IS SOMETHING IN THERE?!
OR SOME*ONE*?

IT STOPPED!

HEY!
WHAT DO YOU
THINK YOU'RE
DOING?

YOU'RE NOT
ALLOWED TO
BE HERE.

THIS
IS PRIVATE
PROPERTY!

SORRY... WE WERE JUST WORRIED.

WE HEARD NOISES COMING FROM THE TANK.

SO WHAT? IT'S ALWAYS DOING THAT.

MOLASSES MAKES NOISE. IT BOILS UP SOMETIMES.

NOW GET OUT OF HERE BEFORE I HAVE TO *HELP* YOU MYSELF.

RUN FOR THE STABLE!

WE CATCH OUR BREATH OUTSIDE.

HAHAHAHAHAHAHAHAHAHAHA

I'M A MOLASSES MONSTER THAT LIVES IN THE TANK! SLIME SHOOTS OUT OF MY EYES!

OR MAYBE IT WAS A SHARK THAT SNEAKED ONTO THE MOLASSES SHIP AND WIGGLED INTO THE TANK THROUGH A PIPE!
I LAUGH, BUT I WISH TONY COULD SEE HOW SMART HE REALLY IS.

MOLASSES DOES COME ON SHIPS FROM ISLANDS IN THE CARIBBEAN.
IT'S PUMPED INTO THE TANK THROUGH A GIANT PIPE. WHO'S TO SAY A SHARK COULDN'T HAVE COME THROUGH?

I DON'T WANT TO SAY WHAT I REALLY THOUGHT WAS HAPPENING—

—WHAT IF A WORKER HAD FALLEN IN AND WAS DROWNING IN THAT DISGUSTING GOO?

NO, THAT'S SILLY. WHY WOULD A WORKER FALL IN?
BUT WAIT UNTIL PAPA HEARS ABOUT THE TANK GURGLING LIKE THAT!

ROSIE!
SHE'S THE ONLY HORSE IN THE STABLE RIGHT NOW, HUH?

NI-NI-NI-NEH
SHE'S TOO OLD TO WORK LIKE THE OTHERS...

BUT MR. VITA LOVES HER TOO MUCH TO SELL HER.

I THINK SHE LIKES MOLASSES EVEN MORE THAN I DO!
SNORT

PAPA? WE'RE HERE!

MRS. GRASSO! WHAT ARE *YOU* DOING HERE?
DID FRANKIE BREAK HIS ARM AGAIN?

CARMEN, *MIA CARA*...I'M SO SORRY.

YOUR PAPA IS VERY SICK.

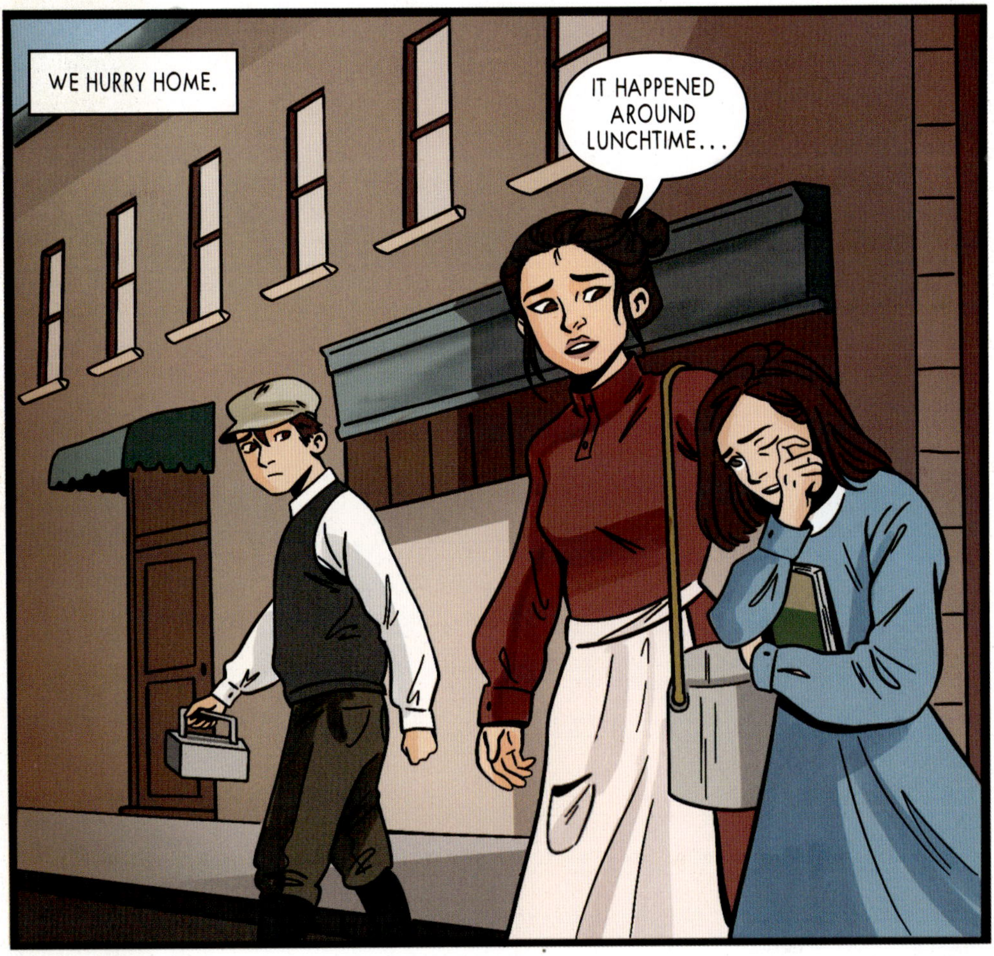

WE HURRY HOME.

IT HAPPENED AROUND LUNCHTIME...

HE'S IN BED NOW.
THE DOCTOR ALREADY CAME.
HE SAID YOUR FATHER HAS SOME KIND OF NEW FLU.
THE FLU? THAT'S NOT TOO SERIOUS.
IT'S NOT LIKE TYPHOID OR RABIES. PEOPLE DON'T DIE FROM THE FLU.
I HAD THE FLU LAST YEAR.
I WAS OUT OF BED WITHIN A WEEK.

PAPA WILL BE FINE...
DEADLY FLU KILLS HUNDREDS
GET YOUR PAPER!
DEADLY FLU KILLS HUNDREDS!

PAPA!

PAPA!

PAPA?

RAGAZZA MIA...

MY GIRL.

PAPA,
I GOT—I GOT
A PERFECT GRADE
ON MY MATH
TEST...

HIS HAND IS
SO HOT!

HE'S
BURNING
UP...
LIKE
HIS BONES ARE
ON FIRE.

I'M HERE,
PAPA.
I'M
HERE.

HOURS PASS.

PAPA MUTTERS IN HIS SLEEP AS THE SUN GOES DOWN.

THEN COMES THE COUGH.
IT'S LIKE LITTLE BOMBS EXPLODING IN HIS LUNGS.

TAKE THIS...
HE'S STILL SO HOT!
I DRIFT BACK TO THE FLOOD AFTER THE EARTHQUAKE...

NONNA HAS TOLD ME THE STORY SO MANY TIMES.

"I WAS UP EARLY THAT DAY BECAUSE THE NAUGHTY GOAT ESCAPED AGAIN.

"I REACHED THE TOP OF THE HILL AND EVERYTHING STARTED TO SHAKE...

RUMBLE

RUMBLE

RUMBLE

RUMBLE

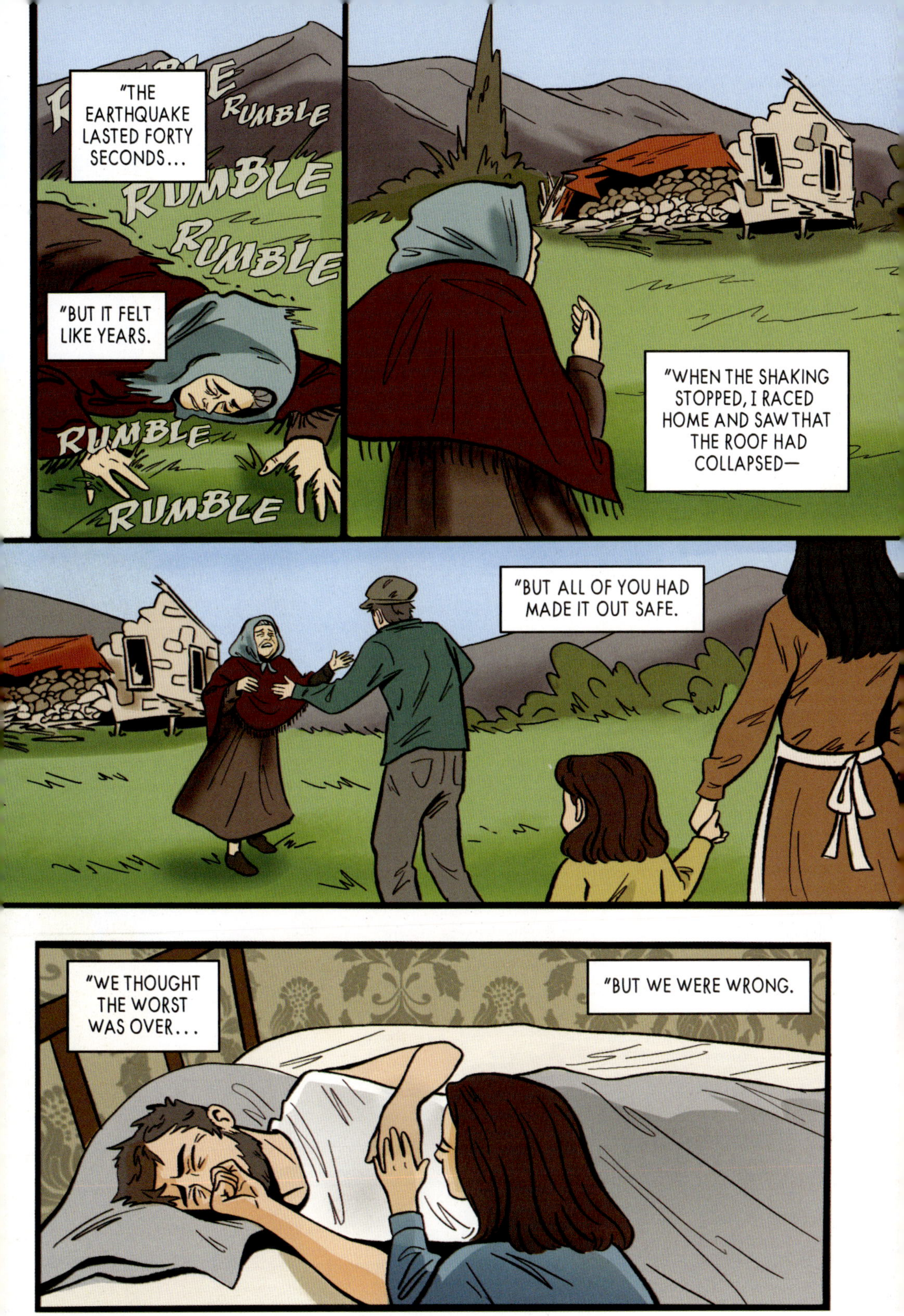

"THE EARTHQUAKE LASTED FORTY SECONDS...

RUMBLE

RUMBLE

RUMBLE

"BUT IT FELT LIKE YEARS.

RUMBLE

RUMBLE

"WHEN THE SHAKING STOPPED, I RACED HOME AND SAW THAT THE ROOF HAD COLLAPSED—

"BUT ALL OF YOU HAD MADE IT OUT SAFE.

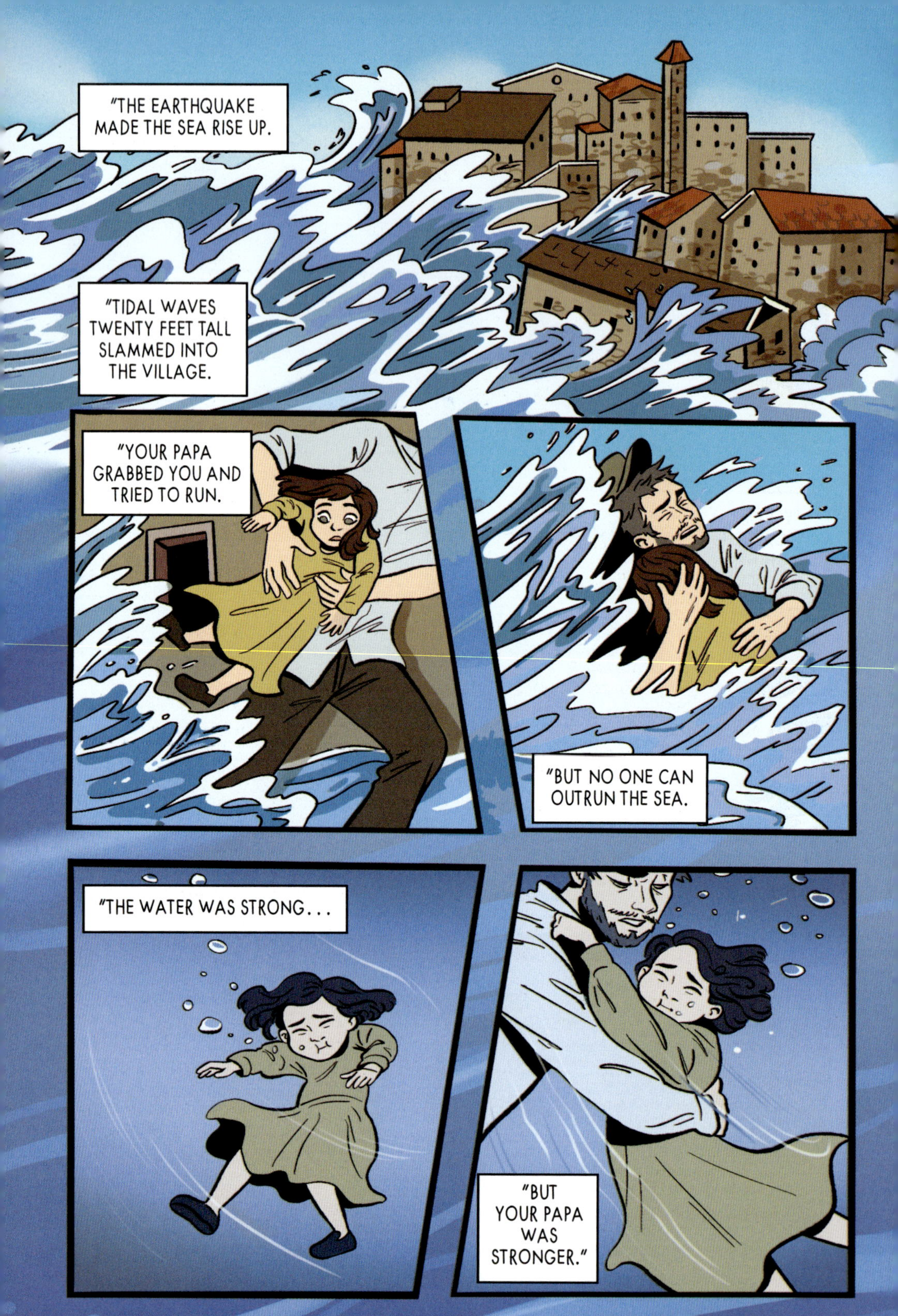

"THE EARTHQUAKE MADE THE SEA RISE UP.

"TIDAL WAVES TWENTY FEET TALL SLAMMED INTO THE VILLAGE.

"YOUR PAPA GRABBED YOU AND TRIED TO RUN.

"BUT NO ONE CAN OUTRUN THE SEA.

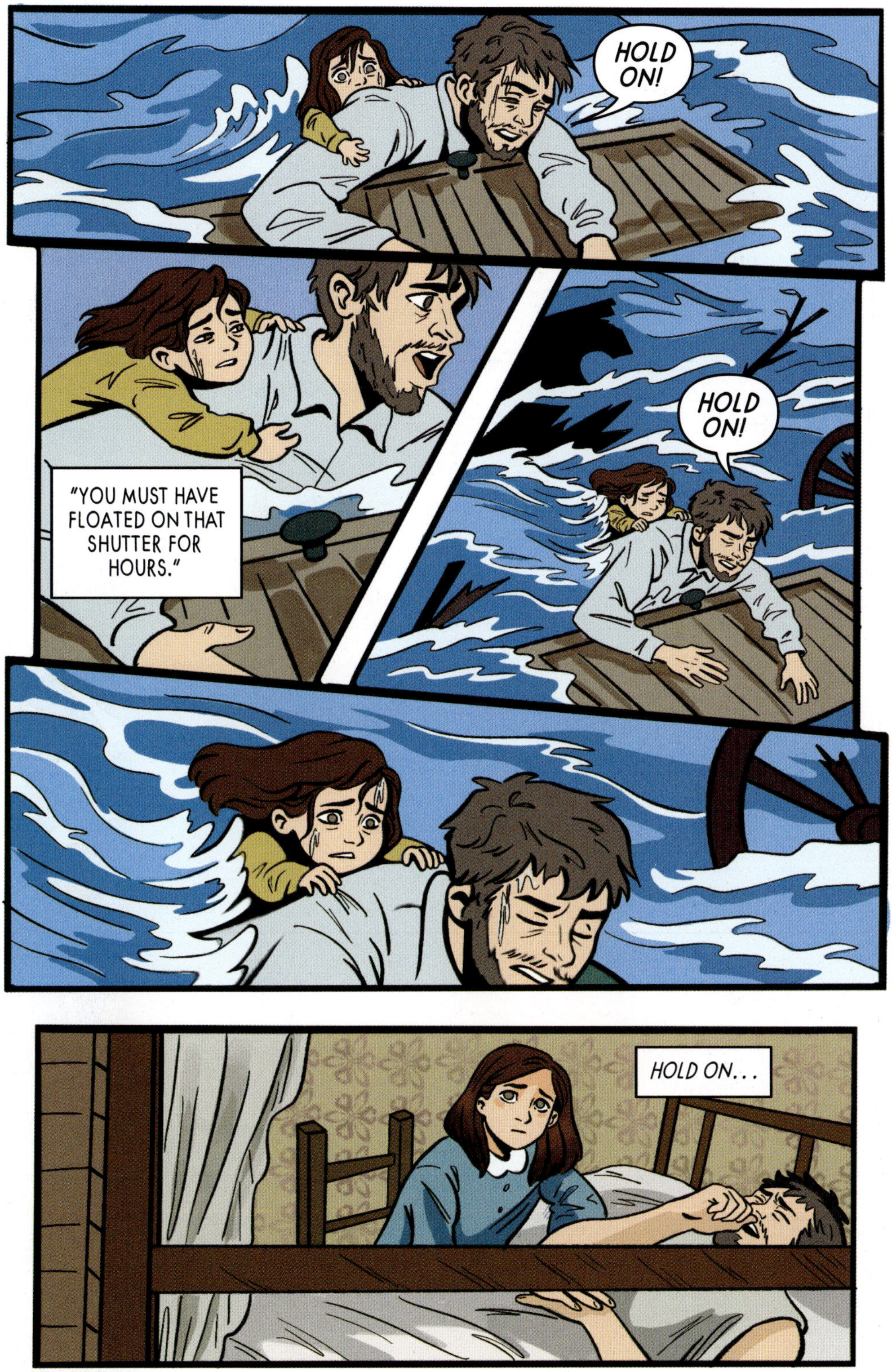

HOLD ON!

"YOU MUST HAVE FLOATED ON THAT SHUTTER FOR HOURS."

HOLD ON!

HOLD ON, PAPA.

PLEASE HOLD ON.

BUT PAPA'S HAND GROWS COLD IN MINE.
SOME THINGS ARE TAKEN AWAY—
—NO MATTER HOW HARD YOU TRY TO HOLD **ON TO** THEM.

Three and a half months later
JANUARY 15, 1919
6:45 a.m.

MORNINGS
ARE ALWAYS
THE HARDEST.

I HEAR PAPA'S VOICE
IN MY MIND...

BUONGIORNO,
RAGAZZA MIA!

GOOD MORNING,
MY GIRL.

GOOD
MORNING...

HI,
CARMIE!

TERESA!

GO BACK TO SLEEP. IT'S STILL EARLY.

THERE'S MARIE . . .

FRANKIE IS ASLEEP ON TONY LIKE ALWAYS, AND SNORING LIKE A GIANT . . . LIKE ALWAYS.
ZZZZ-SNERK-ZZZZZZZZZZ

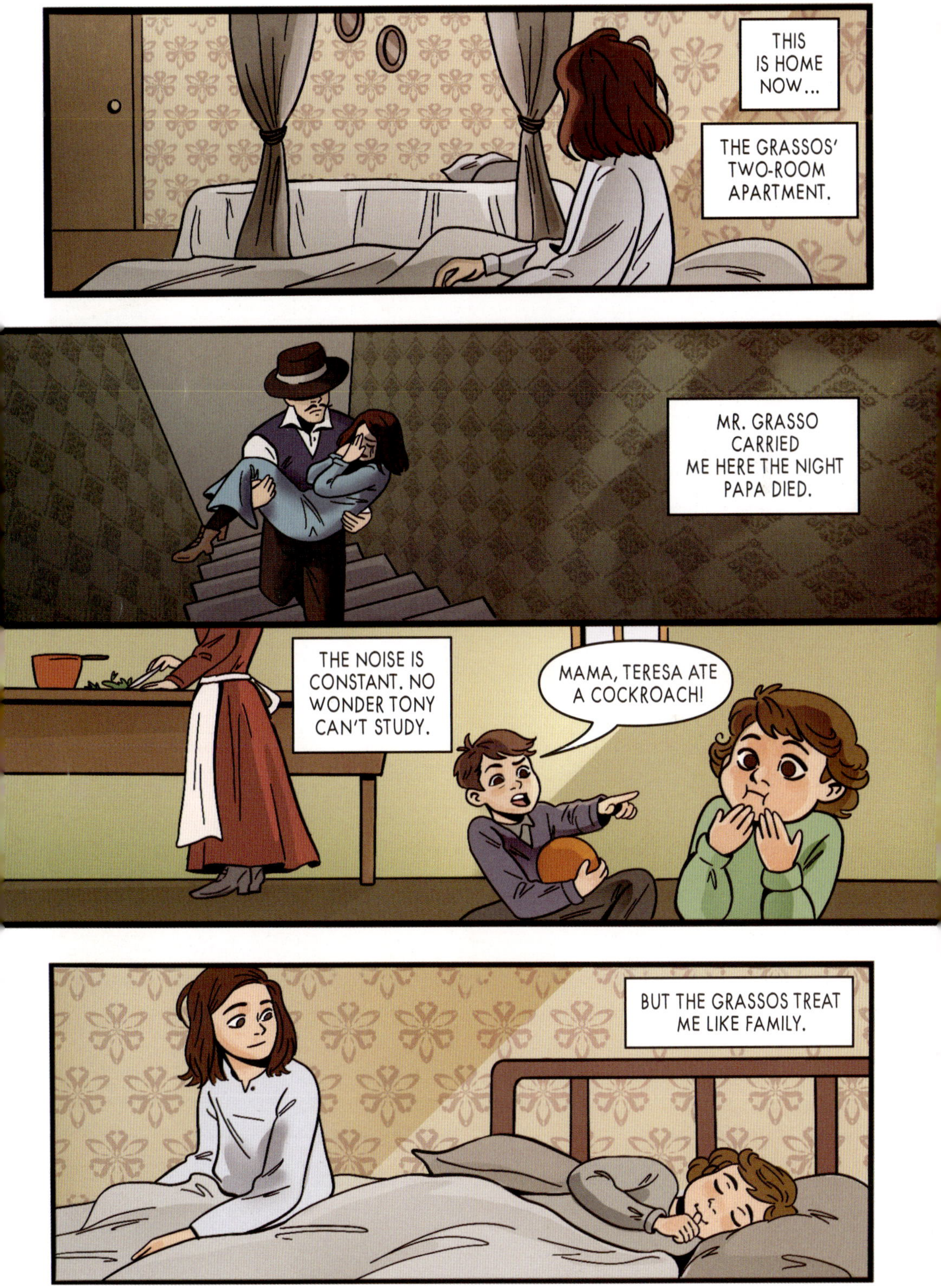

MR. GRASSO CARRIED ME HERE THE NIGHT PAPA DIED.

THE NOISE IS CONSTANT. NO WONDER TONY CAN'T STUDY.

MAMA, TERESA ATE A COCKROACH!

TONY AND FRANKIE ARE LIKE BROTHERS TO ME, AND MARIE AND TERESA LIKE SISTERS.

TONY READS *THE WONDERFUL WIZARD OF OZ* OUT LOUD AT BEDTIME.
HE SAYS IT PUTS THE GIRLS TO SLEEP, BUT I THINK IT'S FOR ME.

I FEEL A LOT LIKE DOROTHY THESE DAYS, LIKE I'M LOST.

BUT THEN TONY TELLS ME A SILLY JOKE—

—OR FRANKIE SHOWS ME HIS NEW BASEBALL CARD.

AND THAT LOST FEELING FADES AWAY.

HELPING MRS. GRASSO IN THE KITCHEN MAKES ME FEEL BETTER, TOO.

WITH SO MANY KIDS, THERE'S ALWAYS WORK TO BE DONE.

THAT TANK!

IT WILL ALWAYS REMIND ME OF THE DAY PAPA GOT SICK.

WE FELT SO CAREFREE.
WE DIDN'T KNOW THAT THE SPANISH FLU HAD SUNK ITS FANGS INTO BOSTON.

IT'S NOT JUST BOSTON, THOUGH.
THIS FLU HAS KILLED PEOPLE ALL AROUND THE WORLD.

"IT'S A PANDEMIC, LIKE THE BLACK DEATH THAT KILLED SO MANY PEOPLE DURING THE MIDDLE AGES.
"OUR HOSPITALS ARE RUNNING OUT OF BEDS."

THERE AREN'T ENOUGH GRAVEDIGGERS TO BURY THE HUNDREDS DYING EACH WEEK.

I'M NOT THE ONLY KID AT SCHOOL WHO HAS LOST A PARENT.
SOME HAVE LOST BROTHERS AND SISTERS, TOO.

SO MUCH HAS CHANGED—
—BUT THAT TANK HASN'T CHANGED AT ALL.

THE GRASSOS GAVE ME NEW BOOTS FOR CHRISTMAS. I'M GRATEFUL—
—THE OLD ONES SQUEEZED MY TOES UNTIL MY TOENAILS TURNED BLACK!

I'LL HELP MRS. GRASSO WITH BREAKFAST. . .
THEN HEAD TO SCHOOL WITH TONY AND FRANKIE—

CARMEN IS A GEM!

THEY'RE TALKING ABOUT ME?

SHE SURE IS.
AND THE KIDS ADORE HER!

WHEN ARE WE GOING TO TELL HER?
NO NEED TO WORRY HER ABOUT THE VOYAGE.

VOYAGE? WORRY?
IT'S SUCH A LONG JOURNEY. IT'S GOING TO BE TOUGH.
ITALY IS VERY DIFFERENT FROM HERE.
I KNOW, BUT IT'S FOR THE BEST.
CARMEN AND HER GRANDMOTHER WILL BE TOGETHER AGAIN.
THEY'RE SENDING ME BACK TO ITALY!

HEY, CARM—
—ARE YOU PRETENDING TO BE A STATUE OR SOMETHING?

THE WICKED WITCH OF THE WEST CAST A SPELL ON HER!

THEY EXPECT ME TO JOIN IN . . .
BUT I CAN'T LAUGH RIGHT NOW.

CARMEN?
I NEED TO GO.

DO YOU FEEL ALL RIGHT?

I'M—
I'M GOING TO SCHOOL.
MR. LAWRENCE WANTED SOME HELP...

SO EARLY? IT'S BARELY SEVEN.

CARMEN?

HOW CAN THEY SEND ME BACK?

IS THIS NONNA'S IDEA? HER LETTERS NEVER SAID A WORD.

THEY KNOW I MISS HER. DO THEY THINK I ***WANT*** TO GO BACK TO ITALY?

GOOD MORNING, CARMEN!
HELLO, MR. PALLO.

LET'S GO, ROSIE.

I'LL HAVE TO
SAY GOODBYE
TO SO MANY
FRIENDS.

WHO WILL
RIDE ROSIE AFTER
I'M GONE?

PAPA ALWAYS SAID. . .
"ANYTHING IS POSSIBLE IN AMERICA.
"IF YOU WORK HARD, YOU CAN BE ANYTHING YOU WANT TO BE."
CLOP
CLOP
CLOP
CLOP

THAT'S NOT TRUE IN ITALY, UNLESS YOU'RE VERY RICH.
THE MEN ARE FARMERS OR FISHERMEN.
THE WOMEN HAVE BABIES.

I WANT A FAMILY SOMEDAY, ROSIE.
BUT I DON'T WANT THAT TO BE MY ONLY JOB.

I COULD BE A NURSE, OR A TEACHER.
OR WRITE A BOOK LIKE *THE WONDERFUL WIZARD OF OZ*.

OUR VILLAGE IN ITALY DOESN'T EVEN HAVE A SCHOOL.

OH, ROSIE...

WHAT WAS I THINKING, ANYWAY?!

THE GRASSOS ALREADY HAVE FOUR KIDS.
MR. GRASSO PROBABLY MAKES LESS THAN THIRTY DOLLARS A WEEK AT THE CONSTRUCTION SITE.

I SHOULD HAVE EATEN LESS! OR TRIED TO FIND A JOB IN A FACTORY!

AND I SHOULD NEVER HAVE ACCEPTED THESE BOOTS...
NEH-NEH-NEH

SORRY, GIRL.

SCHOOL WILL START SOON...
BUT WHO CARES ABOUT MATH OR SPELLING NOW?

THE ONLY MATH I'LL NEED IN ITALY WILL BE FOR COUNTING GOATS.

IT WAS PAPA'S DREAM TO COME TO AMERICA.
BUT PAPA IS GONE NOW.

MAYBE THE GRASSOS ARE RIGHT.
MAYBE IT'S TIME TO GO BACK TO MY OLD LIFE.

MAYBE IT'S TIME TO GO BACK TO NONNA...
I SLIP INTO A RESTLESS SLEEP.

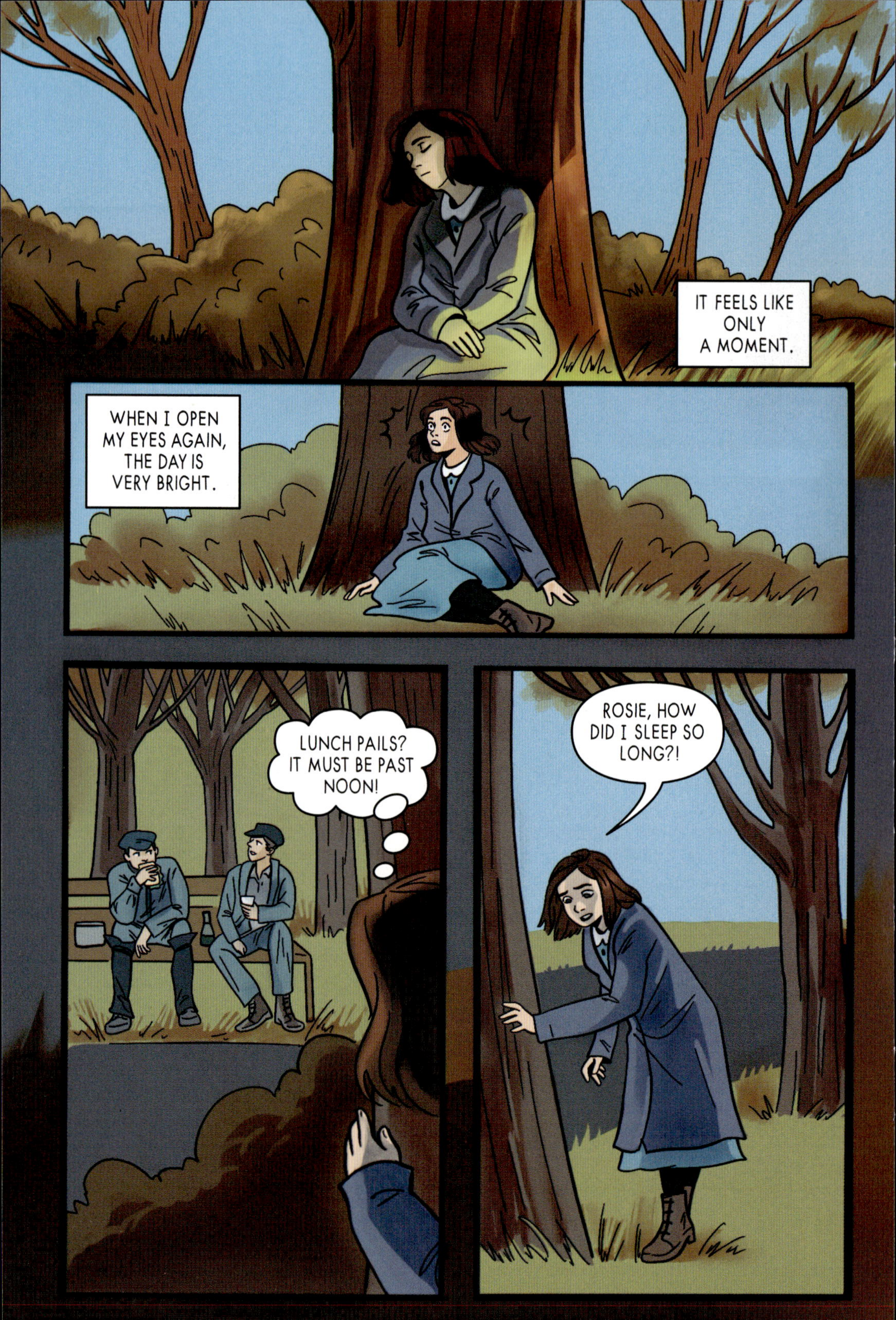

IT FEELS LIKE ONLY A MOMENT.

WHEN I OPEN MY EYES AGAIN, THE DAY IS VERY BRIGHT.

EVERYONE MUST BE WORRIED ABOUT US!
I SHOULD RIDE YOU BACK AND GO TO SCHOOL, OR—

ROSIE?

I DIDN'T TIE HER UP!

WHAT IF SHE GETS HIT BY A MOTORCAR?
HORSES ARE ALWAYS GETTING HIT BY MOTORCARS...

ROSIE!
WHERE IS SHE?
THINK, CARMEN, THINK.

ROSIE IS SMART. WHERE WOULD SHE GO?

BLECH
WHAT'S THAT SMELL?

MOLASSES.

ROSIE!

ROSIE, YOU SMART HORSE!

YOU SMELLED THE MOLASSES IN THE AIR AND FOLLOWED IT RIGHT TO THE TANK.

IT'S ALL OVER YOUR WHISKERS.
SMACK

TRYING TO SAVE SOME FOR LATER?

GRRRRRRR-GLUG-GLUG-
GLUG-GRRRRRRRRRRRR-
GLUG

GURRRR-GLUG-GLUG-
NEVER MIND THAT NOISE, ROSIE.
IT'S JUST MOLASSES BOILING INSIDE THE TANK.
GUH-GURRRRRR

CARMEN!

TONY!

WHERE HAVE YOU BEEN? WE'VE BEEN SEARCHING EVERYWHERE!

I'M SO SORRY...

WHAT CAN I SAY?
DOES HE KNOW ABOUT THE PLAN TO SEND ME TO ITALY?

WE'LL NEVER SEE EACH OTHER AGAIN...
WHAT'S THAT SHAKING?
RUMBLE
RUMBLE
RUMBLE

WHAT'S GOING ON?
SNORT
RUMBLE
AN EARTHQUAKE!
RUMBLE
RUMBLE
RUMBLE RUMBLE RUMBLE
IT'S THE TANK!
RUMBLE
RUMBLE
RUMBLE
GURRRR-GLUG-GLUG-GURRRRRR

THE WHOLE TANK IS ROCKING!
GURRRR-GLUG-GLUG-GLUG-GURRRRRRR
RUMBLE
RUMBLE
RUMBLE

BANG

IT FLEW OFF THE TANK!

BANG
BANG
THOUSANDS OF RIVETS HOLD THE TANK TOGETHER—

—AND NOW THEY'RE ALL LETTING GO AT ONCE!
BANG
BANG
BANG
BANG
BANG

NI-EH-EH-EH-EH-EH
BANG
WE HAVE TO GET AWAY FROM HERE!
BANG
BANG

TONY! GET ON!
SMACK
NEEEEEEEEE-HEE-HEE
HEH-HEH-HEH
ROSIE!

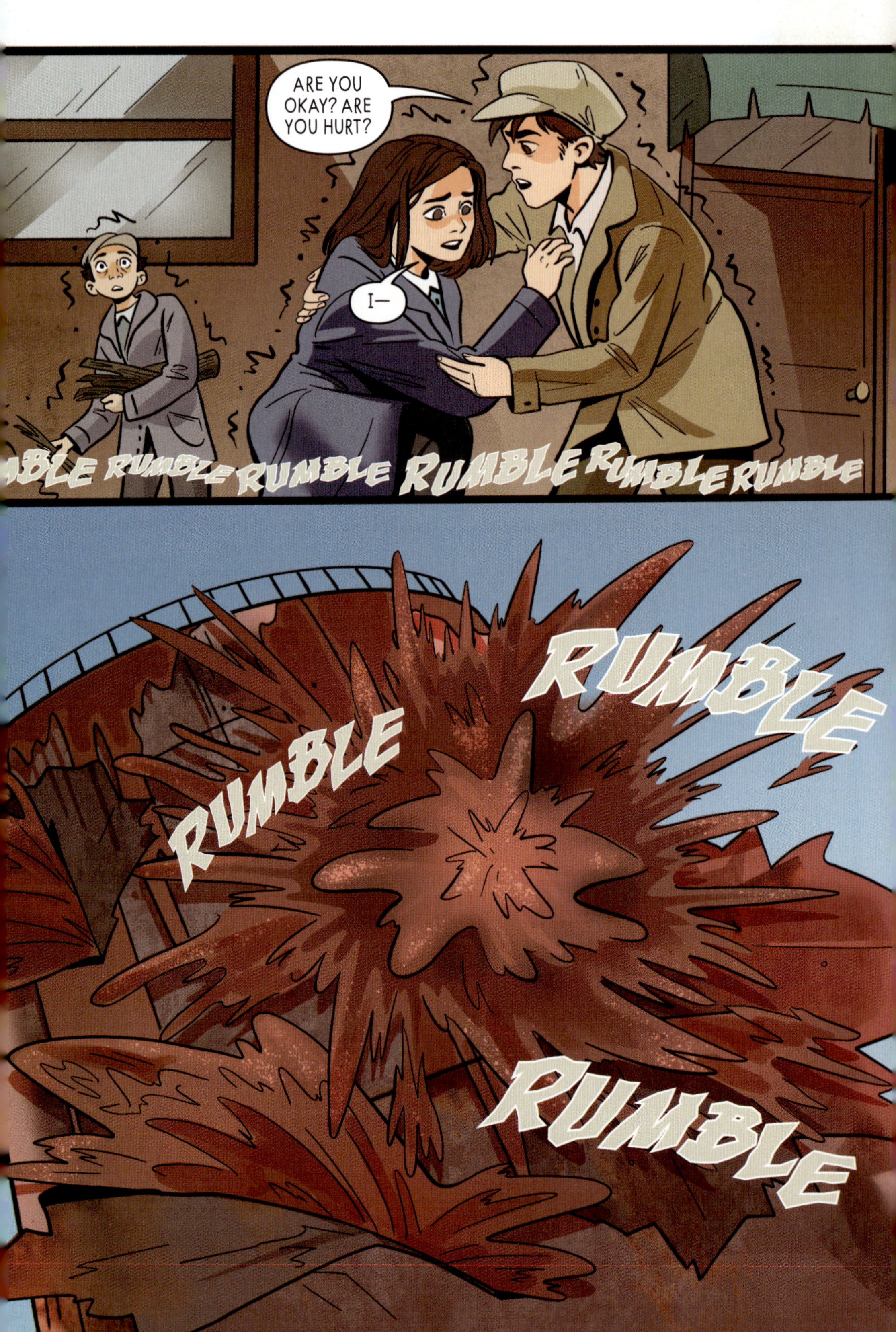
ARE YOU OKAY? ARE YOU HURT?
I—
BLE RUMBLE RUMBLE RUMBLE RUMBLE RUMBLE
RUMBLE
RUMBLE
RUMBLE

RUMBLE
RUMBLE
RUMBLE
RUMBLE
SPLOOOSH
RUMBLE RUMBLE RUMBLE RUMBLE RUMBLE

RUN!

AAAAIIEEEEEEEEE
CRASH
CRACKLE
CRACKLE
NEEEEE-IEEE-EH-
EH-EH-EH
RUMBLE
RUMBLE
RUMBLE

CRASH
IT'S GETTING HIGHER!
WAS THIS HOW PAPA FELT WHEN THE TIDAL WAVE SWEPT US OUT TO SEA?

NO, THIS IS NOTHING LIKE THE SEA...
IT'S HARDENING!
COUGH
COUGH
HACK
COUGH
PAPA FOUND THAT OLD SHUTTER TO FLOAT ON—
THERE!

TONY! GRAB THAT!

UHHH.

UHHH...
OOOF

EVERYWHERE I LOOK . . .
THE MOLASSES SWALLOWS PEOPLE UP.

IS TONY'S FAMILY SAFE?
WHAT ABOUT ROSIE?
WATCH OUT!

CRRRRRRACK

CARMEN!

THE MOLASSES IS LIKE QUICKSAND.
THE MORE I FLAIL...
THE MORE I GET PULLED UNDER.
SCCCRAPE
OWWWWWWW

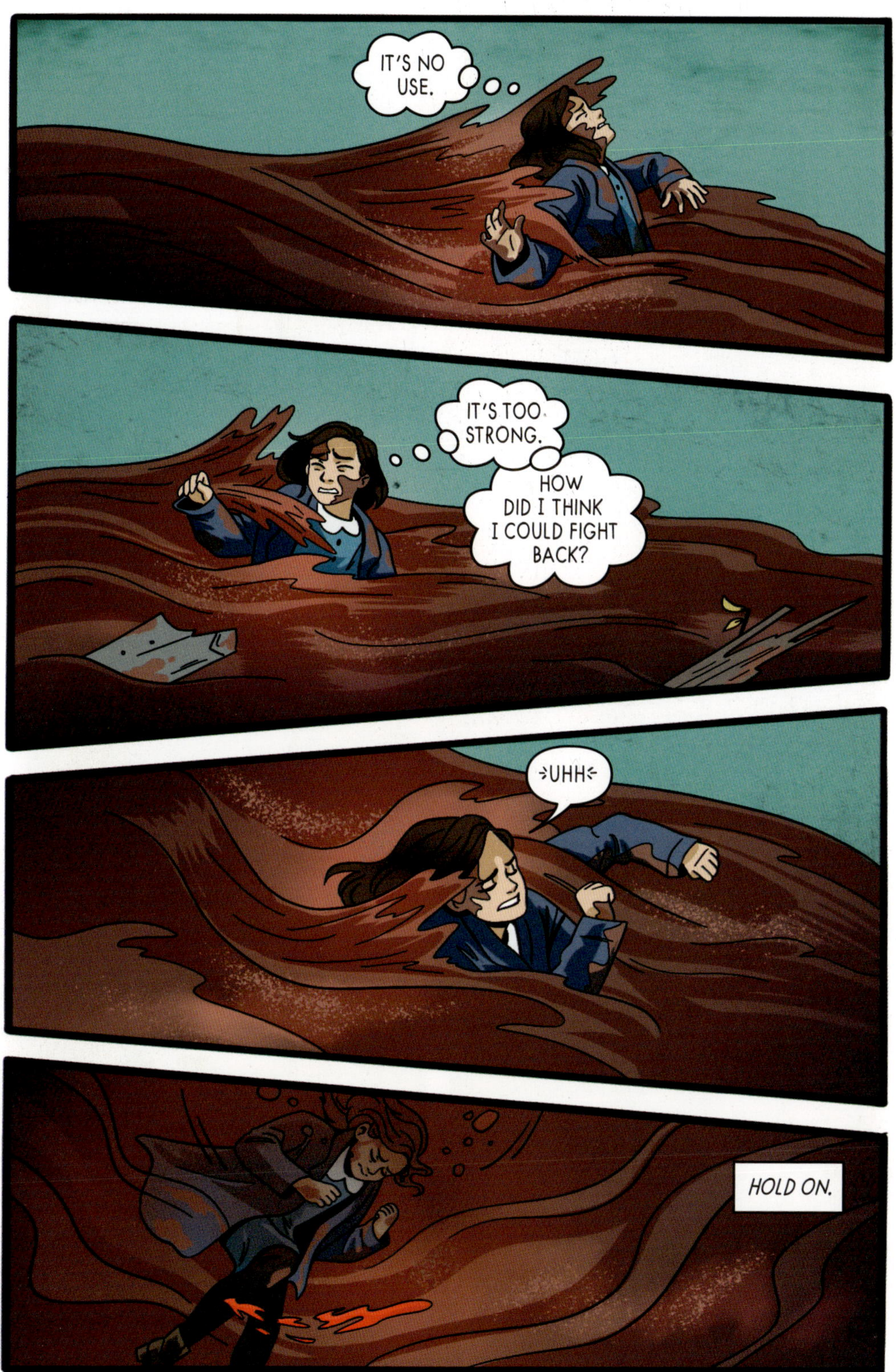
IT'S NO USE.
IT'S TOO STRONG.
HOW DID I THINK I COULD FIGHT BACK?
UHH
HOLD ON.

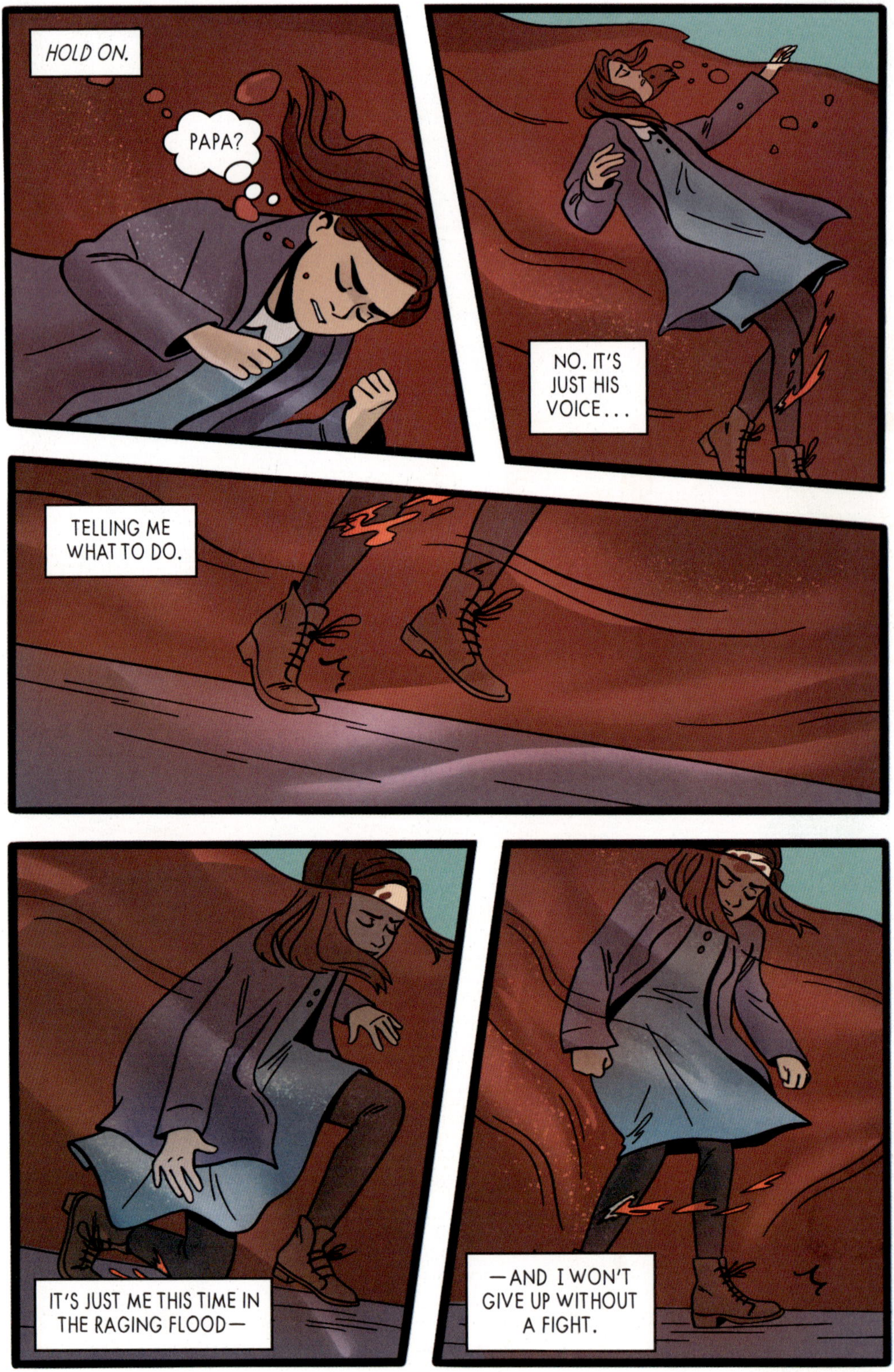

HOLD ON.

PAPA?

NO. IT'S JUST HIS VOICE...

TELLING ME WHAT TO DO.

GASP
HOLD ON.
GASP
I NEED TO OPEN MY EYES NEXT TIME...
FIND SOMETHING TO HOLD ON TO...

HOLD ON.
HOLD ON.

THE WORLD IS BLURRY.
SOUND FADES...
BUT I DON'T LET GO.

An hour later...

SHE'S ALIVE!
CAREFUL, HER LEG IS BLEEDING...

CLEAR HER NOSE SO SHE CAN BREATHE.

PAPA?

DON'T GO, PAPA. . .

Three days later
JANUARY 18, 1919
Around 7:00 A.M.
Boston City Hospital

A SICKLY SWEET SMELL REMINDS ME OF ROT.
LIKE OLD GARBAGE LEFT OUT IN THE SUN—
—BUZZING WITH FLIES . . .
CRAWLING WITH RATS.
HELLOOOOO . . .

HELLO?
MRS. GRASSO?

ARE YOU AWAKE?
NO, NOT MRS. GRASSO...

HELLO, DARLING.
A NURSE.

I KNEW YOU WERE WAKING UP.

DON'T FUSS TOO MUCH, LOVE.

YOU HAVE QUITE A WOUND ON YOUR LEG. LOST QUITE A LOT OF BLOOD.

DOCTORS STITCHED YOU UP THOUGH.

YOU'LL BE RUNNING AROUND SOON ENOUGH.

HOW—HOW LONG HAVE I BEEN HERE?
THREE DAYS?

THREE *DAYS*?!

YOU'RE IN GOOD SHAPE.

AT LEAST COMPARED TO SOME OF THE OTHERS. WHO WOULD HAVE THOUGHT A MOLASSES TANK COULD EXPLODE LIKE THAT?

"THE WHOLE WATERFRONT IS GONE. THEY'LL BE CLEANING UP FOR MONTHS."

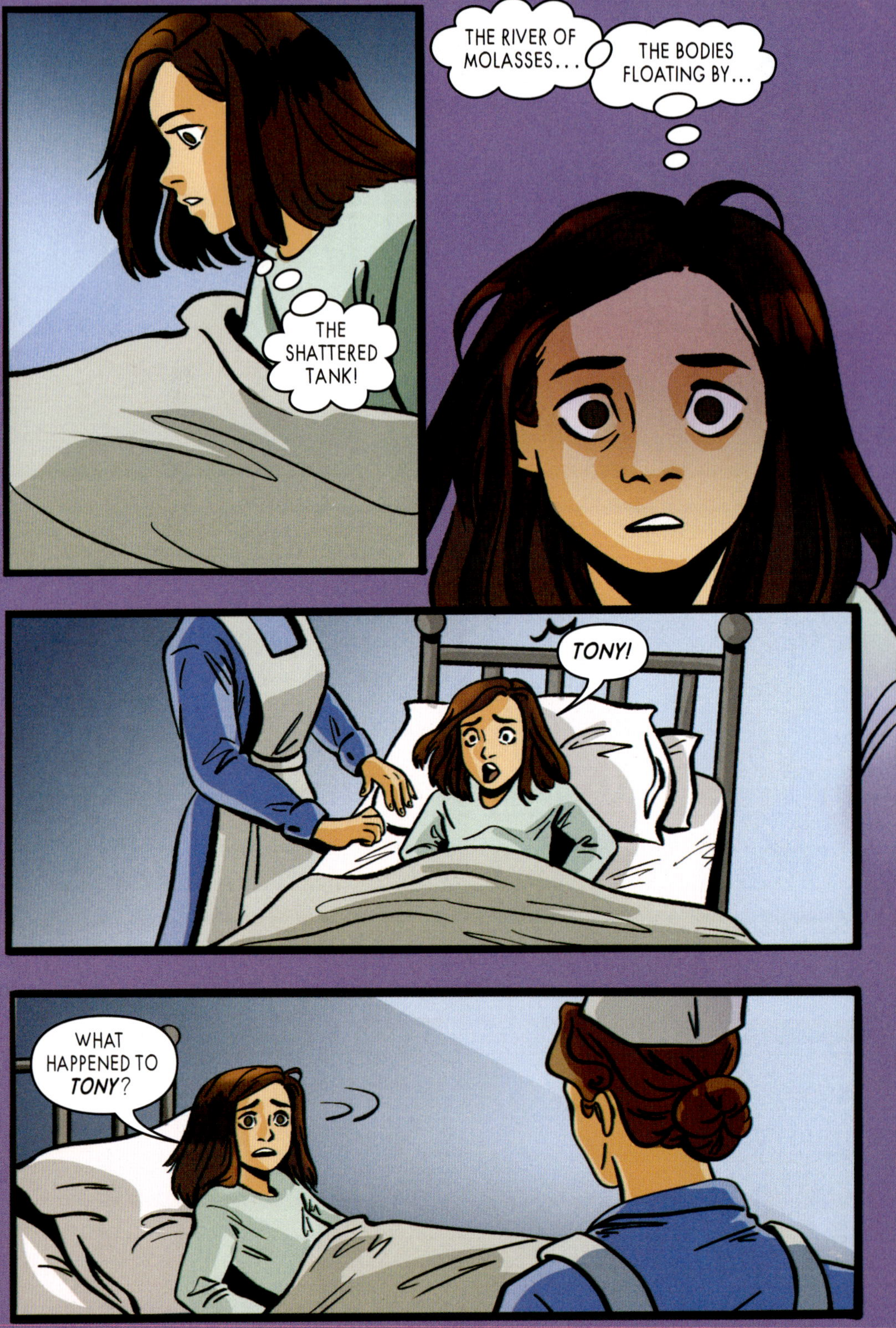

THE SHATTERED TANK!

THE RIVER OF MOLASSES...

THE BODIES FLOATING BY...

TONY!

WHO?
MY FRIEND!

MY **BEST** FRIEND.
NURSE! WE NEED YOU HERE!

DON'T WORRY, LOVE.

YOU REST NOW. I'LL BE BACK.
BUT—

I WANT TO SEE HER FIRST!
NO, ME!
YOU PUSHED ME!
CARMEN!

SHE'S ALIVE!

CARMEN!

WHERE IS HE?!

TONY!

AS THE DAYS GO BY, I GET STRONGER.

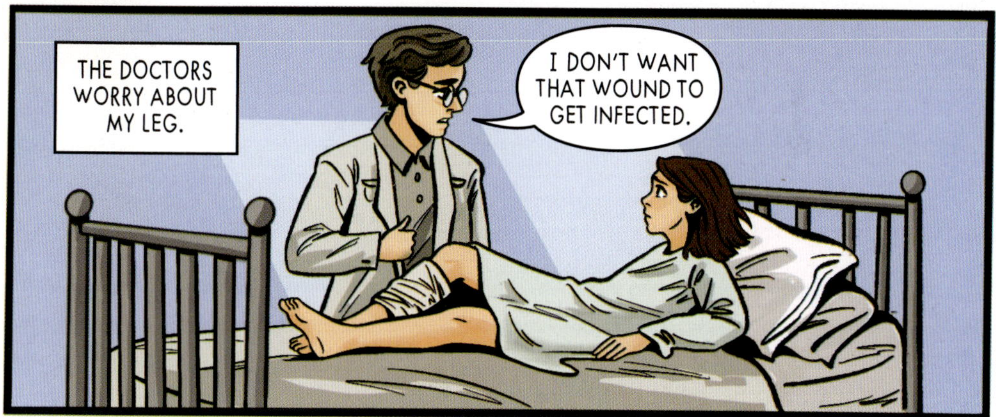
THE DOCTORS WORRY ABOUT MY LEG.
I DON'T WANT THAT WOUND TO GET INFECTED.

YOU'LL NEED TO STAY HERE AT LEAST ANOTHER WEEK.

IF I HAVE TO STAY, AT LEAST I WON'T BE LONELY . . .

MRS. GRASSO COMES BY EVERY DAY WITH PASTA OR LASAGNA.

MRS. ORTELLI BROUGHT A BOX OF CANNOLI AND BISCOTTI FROM THE BAKERY.

I SHARE IT WITH THE NURSES.

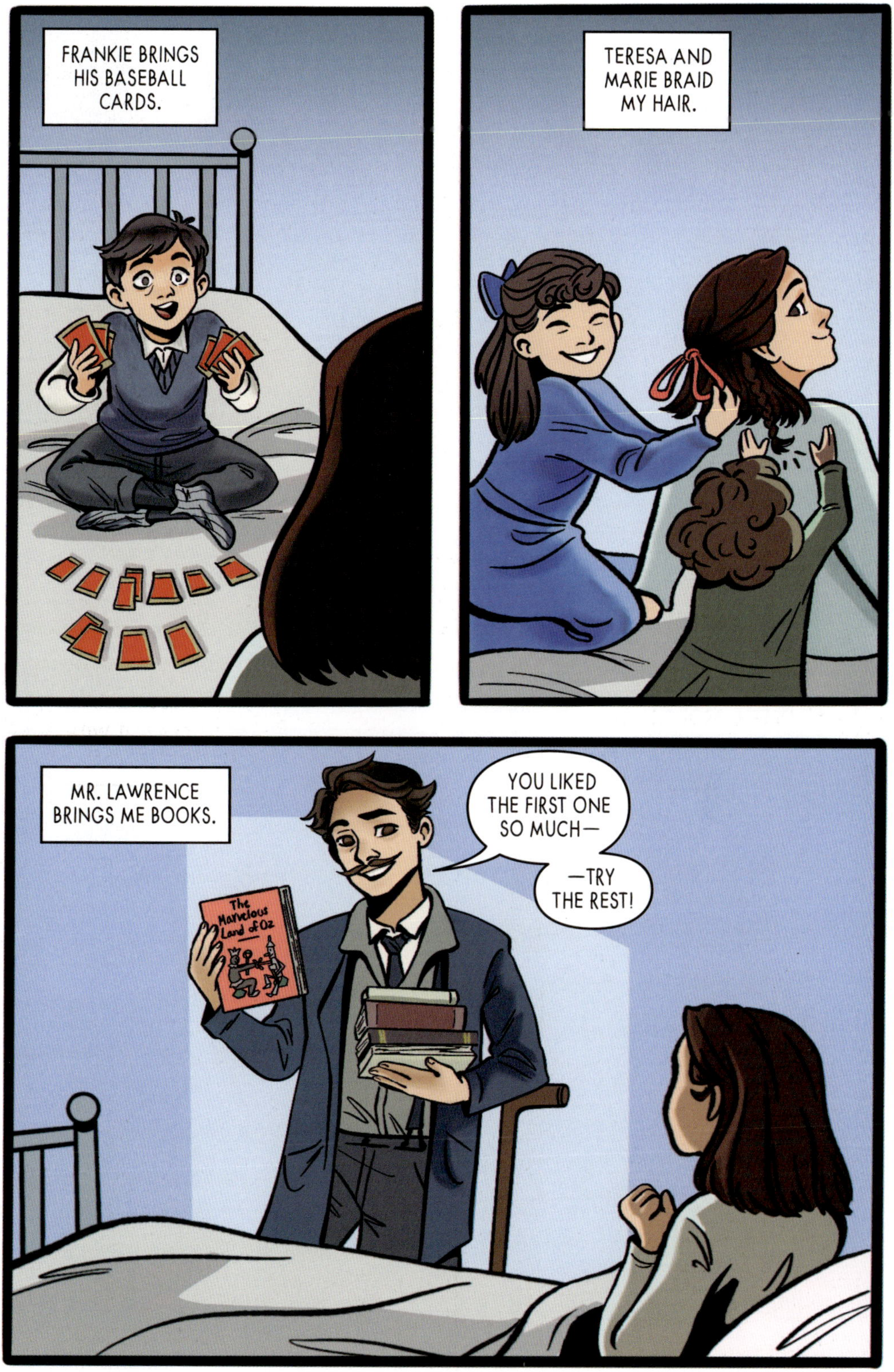

MR. LAWRENCE BRINGS ME BOOKS.

The Marvelous Land of Oz

YOU LIKED THE FIRST ONE SO MUCH—

—TRY THE REST!

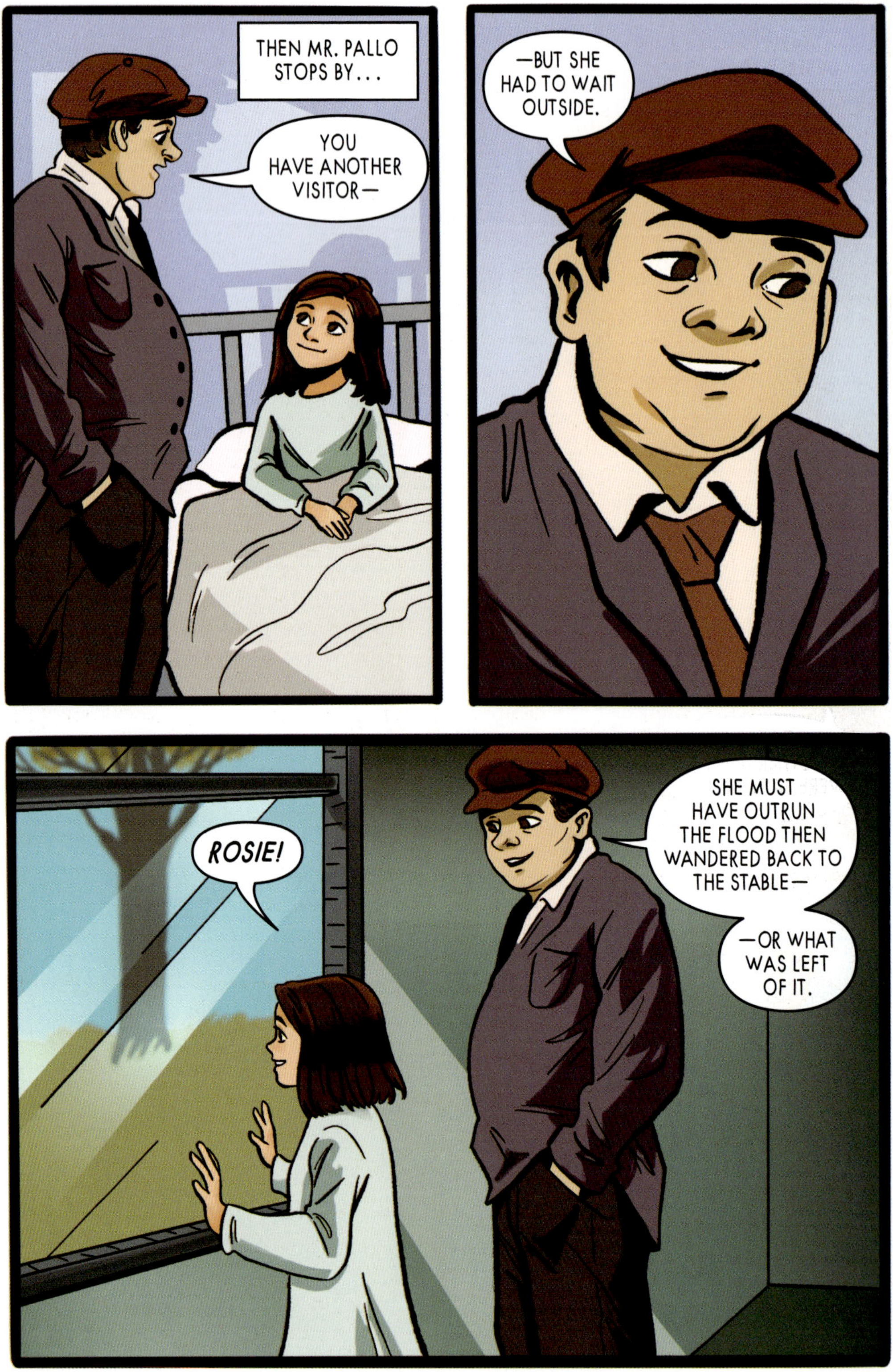

ROSIE!

SHE MUST HAVE OUTRUN THE FLOOD THEN WANDERED BACK TO THE STABLE—

—OR WHAT WAS LEFT OF IT.

THE STABLE WAS DESTROYED.
SO WAS EVERY OTHER BUILDING IN THAT PART OF THE WATERFRONT.

MR. VITA MUST BE SO UPSET ABOUT THE STABLE!
AT LEAST HIS OTHER HORSES WERE SAFE TOO—

—THEY WERE FAR AWAY FROM THE NORTH END WHEN IT HAPPENED.
OTHER HORSES WEREN'T SO LUCKY.

I WAS WORRIED ABOUT ROSIE!
YES, ROSIE IS SAFE.

"AND THAT CUT ON HER NECK IS HEALING UP FINE."

IT'S GOOD TO SEE YOU, GIRL!

NI-I-I-I-
EH-EH-EH

I'M GLAD MR. PALLO BROUGHT ROSIE BY, BUT I WON'T BE ABLE TO RIDE HER AGAIN.

I WON'T BE LEAVING JUST THE HOSPITAL SOON...
I'LL BE LEAVING AMERICA.

NO ONE HAS MENTIONED I'M GOING BACK...
BUT SOMEONE WILL SOON.

MRS. GRASSO HAS PROBABLY ALREADY PACKED MY CLOTHES.

BUT I CAN'T THINK ABOUT THAT.

I NEED TO FOCUS ON GETTING BETTER...

FOR NOW.

OF ALL THE PEOPLE WHO COME TO VISIT, I LOOK FORWARD TO SEEING TONY THE MOST.

AFTER YOU GOT KNOCKED OFF THE CARRIAGE, THE MOLASSES SWEPT ME OFF TOO.

"IT DRAGGED ME OUT TO COMMERCIAL STREET.

"IT GOT SHALLOW ENOUGH FOR ME TO STAND UP AGAIN.

"I SLOSHED AROUND IN A HAZE."

IT WAS TERRIBLE.

"THE BROKEN BODIES WERE SO COVERED IN MOLASSES—
"—I COULDN'T TELL IF SOME WERE MEN OR WOMEN."

"THERE WERE PEOPLE IN PAIN . . .
"INJURED HORSES . . .
"PARENTS SCREAMED FOR THEIR CHILDREN.
"POLICE AND FIREMEN EVERYWHERE.
"MAMA WENT OUT LOOKING FOR ME . . .
"AND FOUND ME PRETTY QUICKLY."

THEN WE LOOKED FOR YOU.
"PAPA WENT TO THE HAYMARKET RELIEF STATION. THAT'S WHERE THEY TREATED LOTS OF INJURED PEOPLE . . . AND WHERE THEY LAID OUT THE BODIES OF PEOPLE WHO DIDN'T MAKE IT.
"THERE WAS THE BODY OF A WOMAN WHO LIVED ON COMMERCIAL STREET.
"AND A GIRL OUR AGE WHO HAD BEEN NEAR THE TANK . . ."
BUT WE DIDN'T FIND YOU THERE.

"MORE THAN ONE HUNDRED AND FIFTY PEOPLE WERE HURT.
"TRAPPED IN CRUSHED BUILDINGS, STRUCK BY FLYING METAL . . .

"THE MOLASSES BLASTED ONE MAN ALL THE WAY INTO THE HARBOR."

THEY TOOK THE INJURED PEOPLE TO HOSPITALS ALL ACROSS THE CITY.

"IT WAS THREE DAYS BEFORE PAPA FOUND YOU HERE IN THE SOUTH END AT BOSTON CITY HOSPITAL."

OH, AND GUESS WHAT—
—THE INDUSTRIAL ALCOHOL COMPANY THAT OWNS THE TANK?

THEY'RE SAYING THE ACCIDENT WASN'T THEIR FAULT.
WHAT?!

THEY SAY SOMEONE PUT A BOMB IN THE TANK.

THOSE LIARS!
SHHH!

EVERYONE KNOWS WHY THE TANK BROKE—

—IT WASN'T BUILT RIGHT!
EVEN FRANKIE AND MARIE KNOW THAT!

I KNOW. DON'T WORRY . . .

NOBODY BELIEVES THE BOMB STORY.

I SURE HOPE HE'S RIGHT.

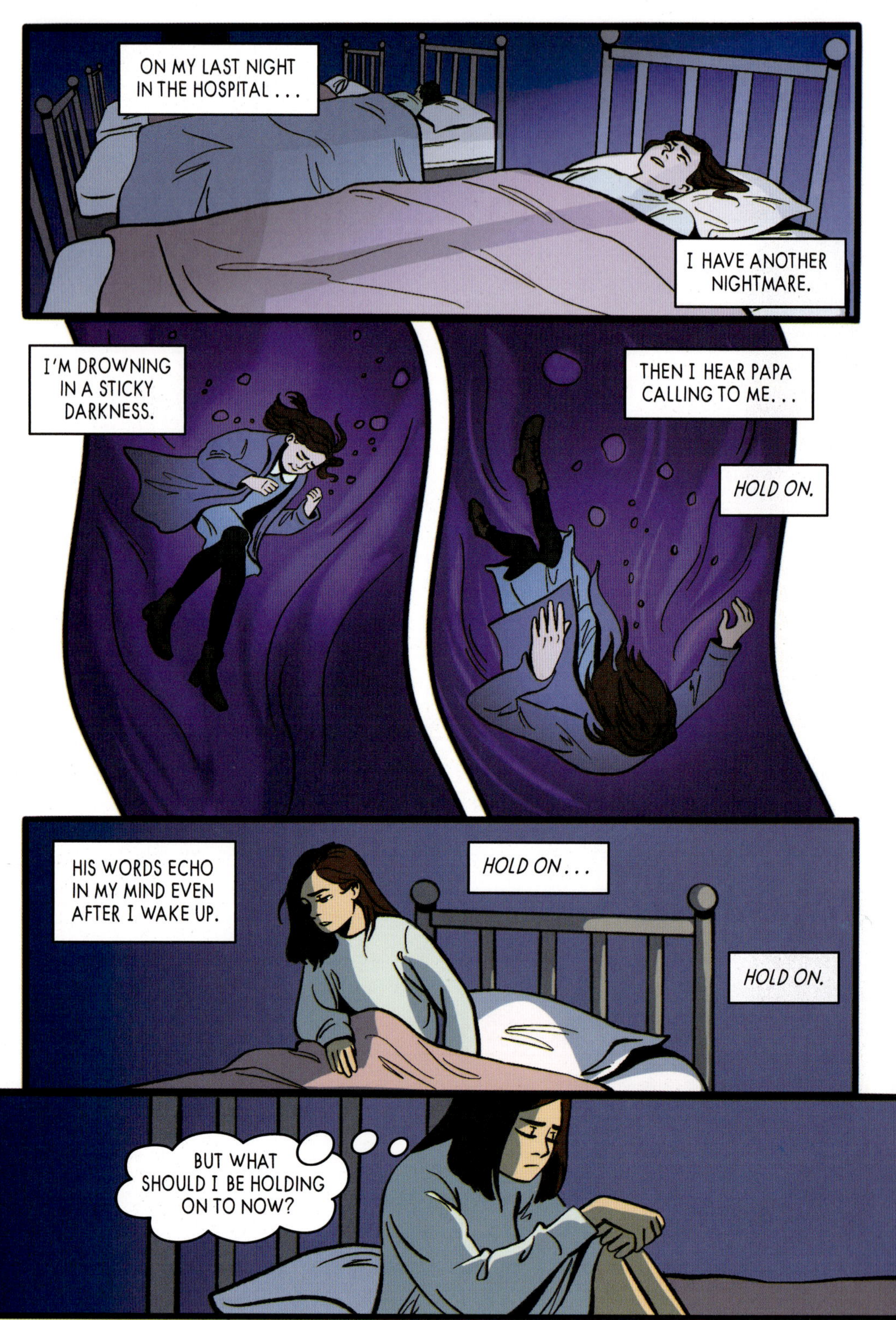

ON MY LAST NIGHT IN THE HOSPITAL . . .
I HAVE ANOTHER NIGHTMARE.
I'M DROWNING IN A STICKY DARKNESS.
THEN I HEAR PAPA CALLING TO ME. . .
HOLD ON.
HIS WORDS ECHO IN MY MIND EVEN AFTER I WAKE UP.
HOLD ON . . .
HOLD ON.
BUT WHAT SHOULD I BE HOLDING ON TO NOW?

SOMEWHERE OUT THERE . . .
THE GRASSOS ARE SLEEPING.
MY SCHOOL IS WAITING FOR STUDENTS TO ARRIVE IN THE MORNING.
MR. LAWRENCE HAS HIS LESSON ALL PLANNED OUT.

HOLD ON.
GASP!
I NEED TO HOLD ON TO THE LIFE WE BUILT IN *L'AMERICA*!
THE SCHOOL I LOVE.
THE FRIENDS WE MADE.
I HEAR YOU, PAPA!

I **CAN'T** GO BACK TO ITALY.

Get Well Soon
IF THE GRASSOS NEED HELP PAYING FOR MY FOOD AND CLOTHES . . .
I'LL FIGURE OUT HOW TO GET A JOB.
IT WILL BE HARD TO WORK **AND** GO TO SCHOOL.
"ANYTHING IS POSSIBLE" DOESN'T MEAN IT WILL BE EASY . . .
BUT I HEAR YOU, PAPA. I WILL HOLD ON.
NO MATTER WHAT.

The next day...

I'M HOME AGAIN.
I DIDN'T PUNCH HER!

I'M BARELY TOUCHING HER!
STOP IT!

THE KIDS ARE BOUNCING OFF THE WALLS.
I'M HUNGRY **NOW**!
I'M HUNGRIER THAN **YOU** ARE!
I'M HUNGRY **MOST**!

THE APARTMENT IS FILLED WITH THE DELICIOUS SMELL OF GARLIC AND CHEESE.

MRS. GRASSO IS MAKING A SPECIAL DINNER IN MY HONOR.
BEST OF ALL, PAPA'S BOSS, MR. VITA, IS GOING TO JOIN US.

HE'S BEEN AWAY, AND MR. GRASSO HAS GONE TO MEET HIM AT THE TRAIN STATION.

WHEN IS MR. VITA COMING WITH CARMEN'S PRESENT?
SHHHH!

THE PRESENT IS A SURPRISE.

I WANT A PRESENT!
MY PRESENT!

BASTA— ENOUGH!

TONY, PLEASE TAKE EVERYONE INTO THE BEDROOM. MAKE SURE THE BEDS ARE MADE.
BUT, MAMA . . .

GO!

I WANT TO HELP . . .

BUT THE DOCTOR ORDERED ME TO STAY PUT.

ALL RIGHT, EVERYONE INTO THE BEDROOM.
BUT, TONY . . .

SOME PEACE AT LAST!

NOW IS MY CHANCE . . .
I NEED TO TELL HER NOW.

I KNOW ABOUT THE PLAN TO SEND ME BACK TO ITALY!

MA VA'!

I OVERHEARD YOU AND MR. GRASSO TALKING ABOUT A VOYAGE.

I KNOW YOU WANT ME TO GO BACK TO ITALY TO BE WITH NONNA.

CARMEN—
I'M SORRY, BUT I'VE DECIDED—

—I WANT TO STAY HERE.

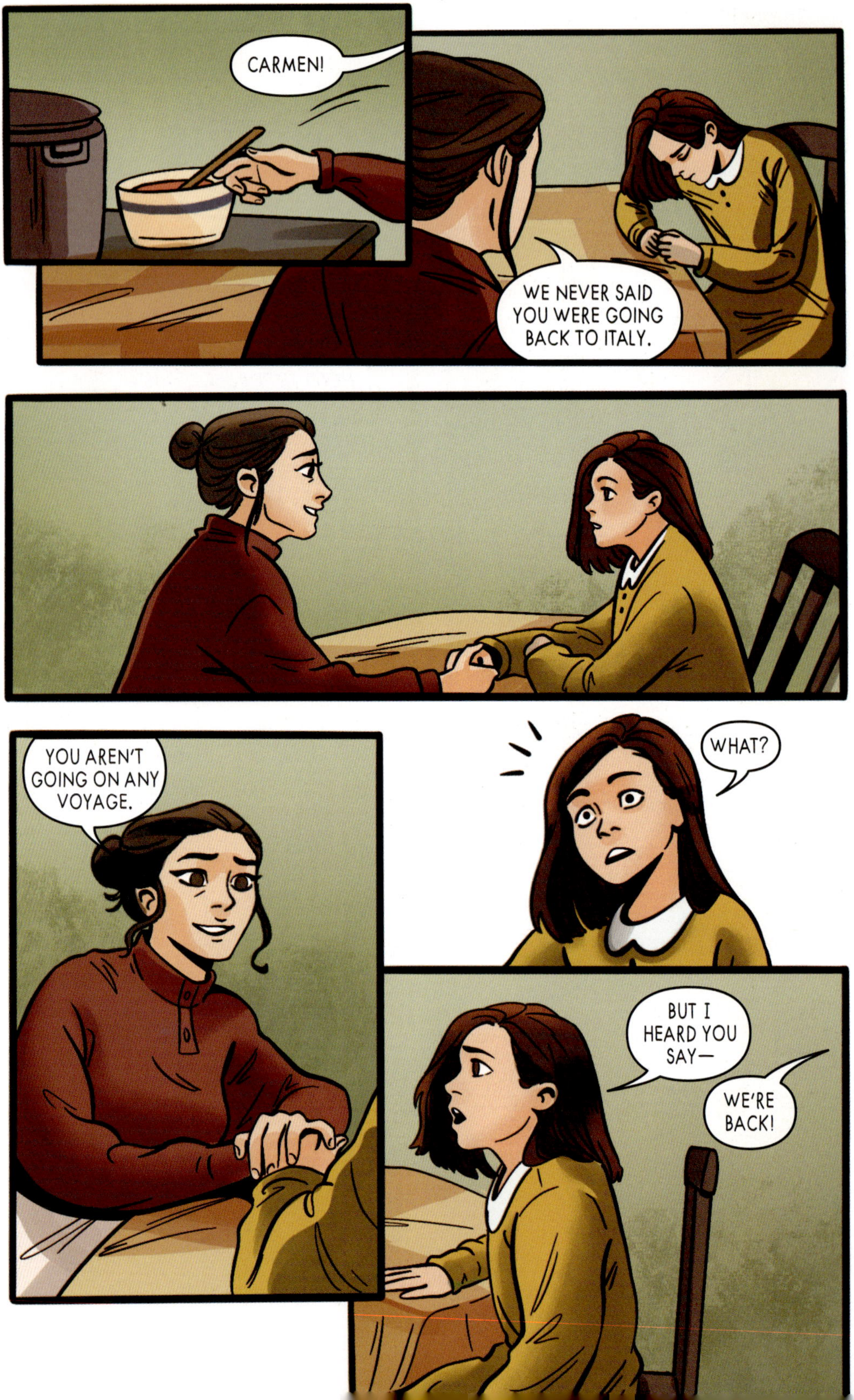

YOU AREN'T GOING ON ANY VOYAGE.

WHAT?

BUT I HEARD YOU SAY—

WE'RE BACK!

SURPRISE!

THEY'RE HERE! THEY'RE HERE!

WHAT'S GOING ON . . . ?

THEY'RE ACTING LIKE BABE RUTH AND THE RED SOX ARE COMING FOR DINNER!

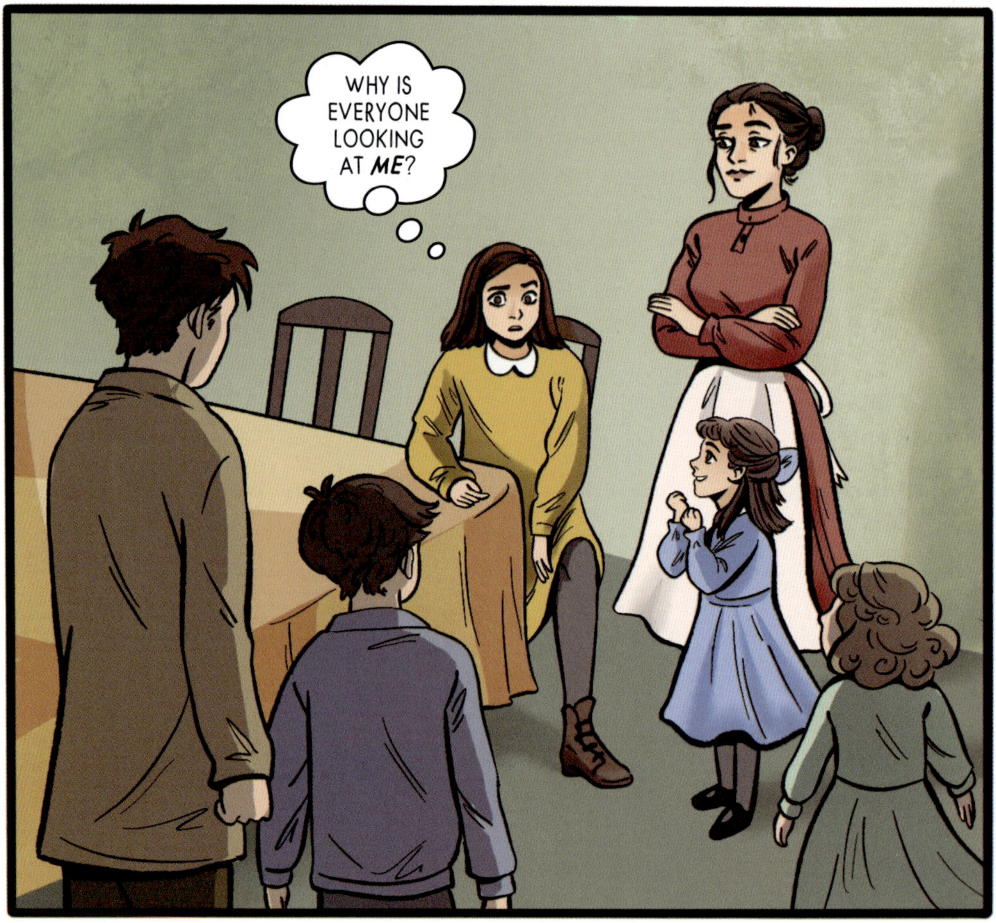

WHY IS EVERYONE LOOKING AT *ME*?

I GLANCE AT THE DOORWAY, BUT I MUST BE DREAMING . . .

NONNA!

LATER, NONNA EXPLAINS.
I MISSED YOU TOO MUCH.

"I WROTE TO MRS. GRASSO.

"MR. VITA CAME TO ITALY TO HELP ME MAKE THE JOURNEY."

DID YOU COME TO BRING ME HOME?

THIS IS YOUR HOME, *TESORA*.

YOUR PAPA BROUGHT YOU HERE.
AND I KNOW HOW SAD THE GRASSOS WOULD BE IF YOU LEFT.

ESPECIALLY THAT *TROTTOLINO*, TONY.

WILL YOU STAY HERE WITH ME?
FOR A WHILE.

WE'LL SEE HOW I LIKE IT.

NONNA SMELLS LIKE LEMONS AND FLOWERS AND THE SEA.
SUDDENLY, I MISS ITALY.

MAYBE I'LL GO BACK SOMEDAY. BUT NOT NOW. AND I WOULDN'T STAY FOREVER.

OR MAYBE NONNA AND I COULD HAVE TWO HOMES WITH AN OCEAN IN BETWEEN . . .

CARMEN,
COME ON!

WE'RE
HUNGRY!
I GET TO SIT
NEXT TO NONNA
AT DINNER!

NO,
I DO!
I DO!

WE'D BETTER
GET OUT THERE,
HUH?

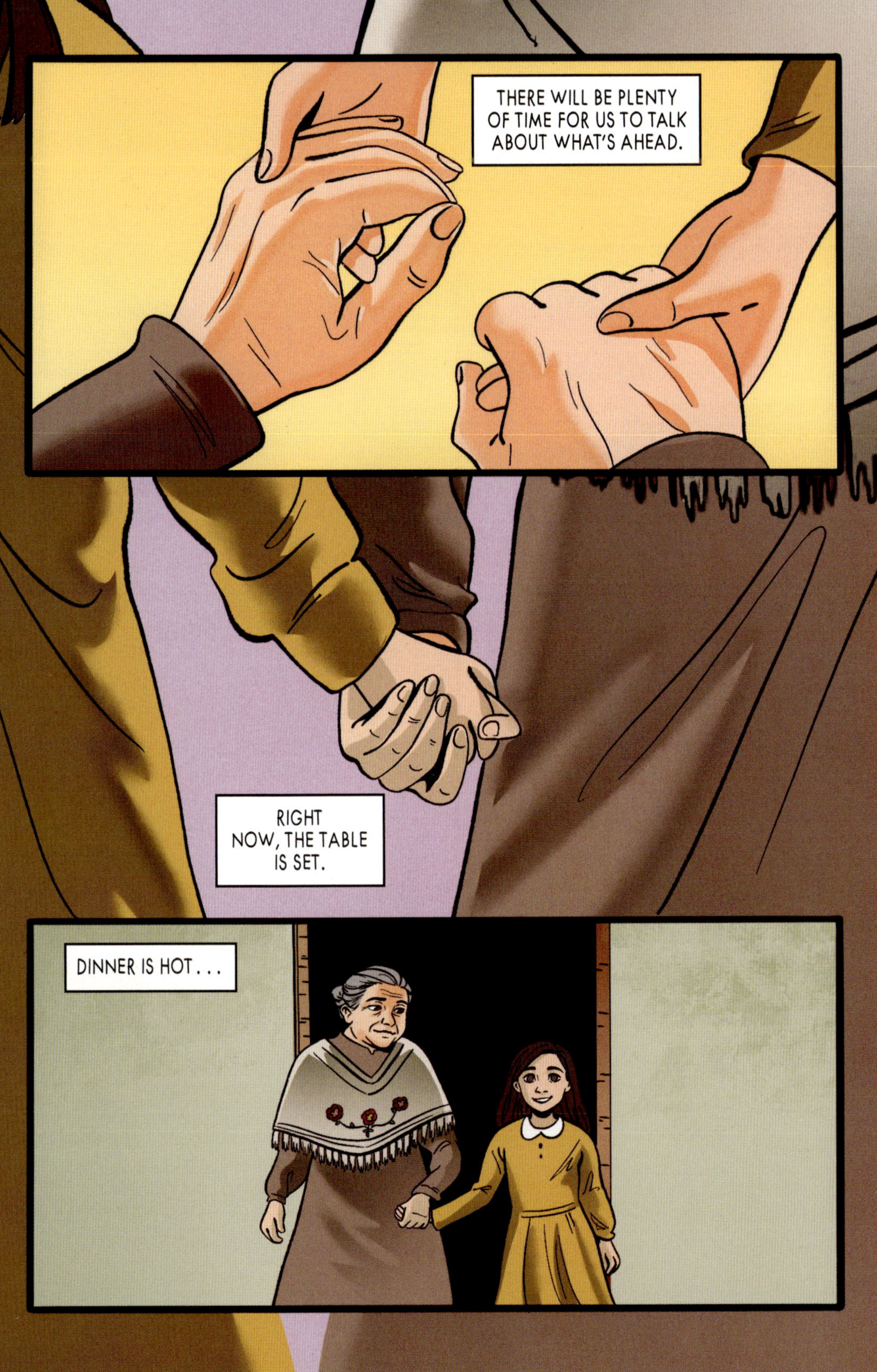
THERE WILL BE PLENTY OF TIME FOR US TO TALK ABOUT WHAT'S AHEAD.
RIGHT NOW, THE TABLE IS SET.
DINNER IS HOT . . .

AND OUR FAMILY
IS WAITING FOR US.

TURN THE PAGE
TO READ MORE ABOUT
THE REAL-LIFE EVENTS OF
THE GREAT
MOLASSES FLOOD, 1919

Dear Readers,

When I first proposed writing about the Boston molasses flood in the I Survived series, my editors weren't so sure about the topic. My other books are about major historical events like the American Revolution, Hurricane Katrina, D-Day, and 9/11. A flood of molasses in Boston? Really?

But as I hope you now agree, the molasses flood wasn't just a strange and sticky accident. It was a tragic event that impacted thousands of people. And as you'll see in the pages ahead, it shaped the world you are living in today. Because of the molasses flood, laws were changed to better protect people from poorly constructed tanks and buildings. Companies that are reckless about safety can be punished for harming people.

And like all my I Survived books, the story of the molasses flood is really a story of people. As I researched this book, I learned so much about the people living in Boston's North End at the time.

Most of them were new arrivals to the United States—immigrants, mostly from southern Italy. They left everything behind to try to build new lives for themselves and their families. Carmen, Tony, and my other characters are all inspired by real people I learned about in my research.

Many of them reminded me of my own immigrant grandparents who came to the United States during that same time—the early 1900s. They faced the same kinds of struggles—hard jobs, cramped apartments, crowded streets, sorrow over the people they had left behind. And just like Carmen and Tony, they were inspired by their dreams for a brighter future for themselves and their families.

Thank you for journeying back in time with me! Keep reading to learn more about life in 1919 America and the molasses flood with Carmen, Tony, and their family to guide you.

Lauren Tarshis

AMERICA WAS CHANGING FAST

WHAT WAS LIFE LIKE IN 1919?

AMERICA WAS IN THE MIDDLE OF A **TRANSFORMATION. NEW INVENTIONS AND TECHNOLOGY** WERE CHANGING HOW PEOPLE LIVED, WORKED, AND TRAVELED.

NEW MEDICINES AND VACCINES MEANT THAT PEOPLE WERE LIVING LONGER.

MORE AND MORE PEOPLE WERE ZIPPING AROUND IN **MOTORCARS**; HORSES WOULD SOON DISAPPEAR FROM THE STREETS OF BIG CITIES.

LIGHT BULBS REPLACED CANDLES AND GAS LAMPS AND MADE HOMES AND STREETS BRIGHTER. THERE WERE NEW WAYS TO HAVE FUN, LIKE GOING TO THE **MOVIES** AND LISTENING TO THE RADIO.

Women fighting for the right to vote were called suffragettes. These suffragettes are on their way to Boston, circa 1913.

FOR YEARS, **WOMEN** HAD BEEN FIGHTING TO HAVE SOME OF THE SAME RIGHTS AS MEN. IN 1919, CONGRESS FINALLY PASSED THE LAW GIVING THEM THE **RIGHT TO VOTE**.

1919 WAS A TIME OF EXCITING CHANGES . . .

THE DEADLIEST YEAR THE WORLD HAD EVER KNOWN

WORLD WAR I BEGAN IN 1914. TENS OF THOUSANDS OF SOLDIERS DIED EVERY DAY IN VICIOUS BATTLES. THERE WERE NEW KINDS OF WEAPONS, INCLUDING MACHINE GUNS AND POISON GAS.

SOLDIERS FOUGHT IN TRENCHES, LONG PITS THAT PROTECTED THEM FROM SOME BULLETS AND EXPLOSIVES. BUT THEY WERE FILTHY, MUDDY, AND RAT INFESTED. SOME SOLDIERS WERE TRAPPED IN TRENCHES FOR MONTHS.

A French World War I sergeant and his dog wear gas masks to protect themselves from poison gas.

NEARLY TWENTY MILLION PEOPLE WERE KILLED IN WORLD WAR I. MANY MILLIONS MORE DIED FROM WAR-RELATED INJURIES AND DISEASES THAT SPREAD DURING THE WAR. ONE OF THOSE DISEASES WAS SPANISH INFLUENZA, WHICH SWEPT ACROSS THE GLOBE AS WORLD WAR I RAGED.

EXPERTS ESTIMATE THAT ONE-THIRD OF PEOPLE IN THE WORLD BECAME INFECTED WITH THE FLU. ABOUT FIFTY MILLION PEOPLE DIED.

THAT'S APPROXIMATELY FIVE TIMES THE NUMBER OF PEOPLE WHO HAVE DIED FROM COVID-19.

675,000 OF THOSE SPANISH FLU DEATHS WERE IN THE UNITED STATES.

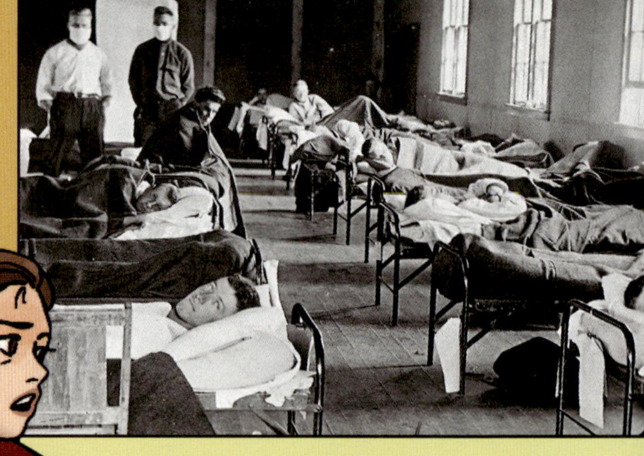

Spanish flu victims in 1918

MOLASSES IN AMERICA

BUT WHAT DOES ALL THAT HAVE TO DO WITH MOLASSES?

PRIOR TO WORLD WAR I, MOLASSES WAS MOSTLY USED AS A **SWEETENER** IN FOOD, THE WAY WE USE SUGAR TODAY. (MOLASSES IS MADE FROM THE SAME PLANT AS SUGAR BUT WAS CHEAPER THAN SUGAR AT THE TIME.)

BUT BY 1919, MOST MOLASSES IN AMERICA WAS USED TO MAKE **INDUSTRIAL ALCOHOL**, A KEY INGREDIENT IN **BOMBS AND EXPLOSIVES**. THESE WEAPONS WERE NEEDED FOR WORLD WAR I.

A tin of molasses candy from 1910

THE DISASTER

THE TANK IN BOSTON'S NORTH END EXPLODED APART ON JANUARY 15, 1919, AT ABOUT 12:30 P.M. IT TOOK LESS THAN **FIVE MINUTES** FOR THE **MASSIVE WAVE OF MOLASSES** TO COAT THE NEIGHBORHOOD. SEVERAL BUILDINGS WERE KNOCKED DOWN. BUILDINGS, VEHICLES, ANIMALS, AND PEOPLE WERE SWEPT AWAY.

A section of the tank after the flood

AT ITS PEAK, THE WAVE REACHED A HEIGHT OF **40 FEET** AND SPREAD AT A RATE OF **35 MILES PER HOUR**. SEVERAL CITY BLOCKS WERE DROWNED IN A LAYER OF GOO TWO- TO THREE-FEET DEEP. THE STICKY WAVE TOOK THE LIVES OF **21 PEOPLE**, INCLUDING TWO CHILDREN. IT ALSO INJURED 150 PEOPLE, MANY SERIOUSLY.

THE CLEANUP

Rescue workers swarm the North End waterfront after the flood.

WITHIN MINUTES OF THE DISASTER, THE NORTH END WATERFRONT WAS SWARMING WITH POLICE, FIREFIGHTERS, DOCTORS, NURSES, SAILORS FROM SHIPS IN THE HARBOR, AND OTHER **RESCUE WORKERS**.

THEY WORKED AROUND THE CLOCK **SEARCHING FOR VICTIMS**. THEY FOUND THEM BURIED IN THE WRECKAGE OF BUILDINGS, TRAPPED IN MOLASSES-FLOODED BASEMENTS, AND TANGLED UP WITH TWISTED METAL AND WRECKED RAILCARS AND WAGONS.

WHAT MADE THE RESCUE EFFORTS MORE DIFFICULT IS THAT **THE MOLASSES HARDENED**. RESCUERS HAD TO USE PICKS AND CHISELS TO FREE SOME OF THE BODIES.

Firemen stand knee-deep in molasses.

CLEANING UP WAS AN ENORMOUS CHALLENGE. MOLASSES WAS EVERYWHERE—IN BASEMENTS, POOLED IN THE STREETS, HARDENED INTO A THICK CRUST ON THE SIDEWALKS.

A worker uses a torch to cut through part of the fallen tank.

PLAIN WATER DID LITTLE TO WASH THE MOLASSES AWAY. FINALLY, FIREFIGHTERS USED A FIREBOAT TO SPRAY **MILLIONS OF GALLONS OF SALT WATER** FROM THE HARBOR ONTO THE STREETS AND SIDEWALKS. THE SALT LOOSENED THE MOLASSES SO WORKERS COULD SCRUB IT OFF.

IT TOOK ABOUT SIX MONTHS FOR THE WRECKAGE TO BE CLEARED AWAY . . .

DOOMED FROM THE START

FROM THE START, IT WAS OBVIOUS WHO CAUSED THIS DISASTER: THE COMPANY THAT OWNED THE TANK, **UNITED STATES INDUSTRIAL ALCOHOL** (USIA). THEY WERE IN A RUSH TO BUILD THE TANK. THEY DIDN'T TEST IT PROPERLY AFTER IT WAS BUILT. THEY IGNORED THREE YEARS OF LEAKS.

The tank before it burst

A man sweeps the street in the North End, not far from the tank.

ONE OF THEIR OWN WORKERS, ISAAC GONZALEZ, WAS SO WORRIED THAT HE HAD NIGHTMARES. HE WARNED HIS BOSSES, BUT THEY DIDN'T LISTEN. **MANY PEOPLE WHO LIVED AND WORKED** AROUND THE TANK KNEW THAT IT WAS DANGEROUS AND THAT ONE DAY A DISASTER COULD HAPPEN.

HOLDING USIA RESPONSIBLE

BUT AFTER THE DISASTER, USIA REFUSED TO ADMIT THAT THE TANK WAS **POORLY BUILT**. THEY TRIED TO CONVINCE PEOPLE THAT SOMEONE HAD THROWN **DYNAMITE** INTO THE TANK, CAUSING IT TO EXPLODE.

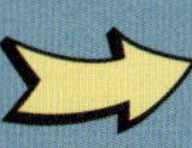

VICTIMS OF THE FLOOD AND THEIR FAMILIES GOT TOGETHER AND SUED USIA. A JUDGE DECIDED THAT **USIA SHOULD PAY** A TOTAL OF ABOUT **$693,000** TO THE FLOOD'S VICTIMS. TODAY, THAT MONEY WOULD BE WORTH ABOUT TEN MILLION DOLLARS.

TANK DISASTER CASE IS ENDED

Agreement Reached With Plaintiffs Out of Court

U. S. Industrial Alcohol Co to Pay $500,000 to $1,000,000

Damage Due to Collapse of Molasses Container

A case at law which is said to have ... the most extraordinary in the ... State was brought to final ... when Judge ... considera... the

THIS WAS ONE OF THE FIRST TIMES IN THE UNITED STATES THAT A BUSINESS HAD BEEN FORCED TO PAY VICTIMS WHEN IT **CAUSED A DEADLY DISASTER**.

THE FLOOD MADE US SAFER

TODAY, IF YOU OWNED A COMPANY THAT WANTED TO BUILD A GIANT TANK, YOU WOULD NEED TO FIRST GET A PERMIT FROM THE CITY. YOUR PLAN WOULD HAVE TO BE **APPROVED BY ENGINEERS**.

Engineers review building plans to make sure they're safe.

Workers for OSHA, a government agency that makes sure buildings are safe

IN OTHER WORDS, THERE ARE LAWS TO MAKE SURE THAT NOBODY BUILDS A TANK—OR A BUILDING, HOUSE, OR FACTORY—THAT ISN'T **SAFE**.

BOSTON'S NORTH END IS STILL A **VIBRANT COMMUNITY** THAT CELEBRATES THE ITALIAN CULTURE OF MANY OF ITS RESIDENTS, JUST LIKE IT DID IN CARMEN AND TONY'S TIME. AROUND EVERY CORNER, YOU'LL FIND SCRUMPTIOUS ITALIAN PASTRIES AND AUTHENTIC PIZZA AND PASTA.

Italian flags decorate a street in Boston's North End.

THE FLOOD IS STILL REMEMBERED BY THE COMMUNITY. THE NORTH END HAS A PLAQUE HONORING THOSE WHO DIED IN THE FLOOD. SOME LONGTIME RESIDENTS CLAIM THEY CAN **STILL SMELL THE MOLASSES**.

FURTHER READING

Some books you can read about the molasses flood and that time in history:

Harlow, Joan Hiatt. *Joshua's Song*. New York: Simon & Schuster, 2001.

Kops, Deborah. *The Great Molasses Flood*. Watertown, MA: Charlesbridge, 2012.

SELECTED BIBLIOGRAPHY

Barry, John M. *The Great Influenza: The Story of the Deadliest Pandemic in Human History*. New York: Penguin Group, 2004.

Bureau of Labor Statistics. "The Life of American Workers in 1915," *Monthly Labor Review*, February 2016.

Jabr, Ferris. "The Science of the Great Molasses Flood," *Scientific American*, August 1, 2013.

Keller, Jared. "How the Boston Molasses Flood Ushered in the Era of Modern Regulation," *Pacific Standard*, January 7, 2019.

Laskin, David. *The Long Way Home*. New York: HarperCollins, 2010.

Press, Julia. "A Deadly Tsunami of Molasses in Boston's North End," NPR, January 15, 2019.

Puleo, Stephen. *Dark Tide: The Great Boston Molasses Flood of 1919*. Boston: Beacon Press, 2003.

Puleo, Stephen. *The Boston Italians*. Boston: Beacon Press, 2007.

University of Michigan Center for the History of Medicine and Michigan Publishing. "Boston, Massachusetts," *American Influenza Epidemic of 1918–1919: A Digital Encyclopedia*, University of Michigan Library.

LAUREN TARSHIS'S

NEW YORK TIMES BESTSELLING I SURVIVED SERIES TELLS STORIES OF YOUNG PEOPLE AND THEIR RESILIENCE AND STRENGTH IN THE MIDST OF UNIMAGINABLE DISASTERS AND TIMES OF TURMOIL. LAUREN HAS BROUGHT HER SIGNATURE WARMTH AND EXHAUSTIVE RESEARCH TO TOPICS SUCH AS THE BATTLE OF D-DAY, THE AMERICAN REVOLUTION, HURRICANE KATRINA, THE BOMBING OF PEARL HARBOR, AND OTHER WORLD EVENTS. SHE LIVES IN CONNECTICUT WITH HER FAMILY AND CAN BE FOUND ONLINE AT LAURENTARSHIS.COM.

GEORGIA BALL

HAS WRITTEN COMICS FOR MANY OF HER FAVORITE CHILDHOOD CHARACTERS, INCLUDING STRAWBERRY SHORTCAKE, TRANSFORMERS, LITTLEST PET SHOP, MY LITTLE PONY, AND THE DISNEY PRINCESSES. IN ADDITION TO ADAPTING LAUREN TARSHIS'S I SURVIVED SERIES TO GRAPHIC NOVELS, GEORGIA WRITES ABOUT HISTORICAL EVENTS SUCH AS THE WORLD WAR II BATTLES OF KURSK AND GUADALCANAL. GEORGIA LIVES WITH HER HUSBAND, DAUGHTER, AND RAMBUNCTIOUS PETS IN FLORIDA. VISIT HER ONLINE AT GEORGIABALLAUTHOR.COM.

KAREN DE LA VEGA

WAS BORN AND RAISED IN THE NORTHERN MOUNTAINOUS CITY OF MONTERREY, NUEVO LEÒN, MÈXICO. *DREAMER*, HER FIRST PUBLISHED WORK, WAS A 2024 YALSA NOMINEE FOR GREAT GRAPHIC NOVELS FOR TEENS.

NEDA KAZEMIFAR

IS A NEW YORK–BASED COLOR ARTIST AND ILLUSTRATOR KNOWN FOR HER WORK ON ACCLAIMED SERIES SUCH AS PRIYA AND THE LOST GIRLS AND JUPITER INVINCIBLE. DISCOVER HER PORTFOLIO AT FINIFACTORY.COM.